GPST STAGE 2
Clinical Problem Solving

1400 EMQs
FOR GPST/GPVTS ENTRY

Nishali Patel MBBS BSc nMRCGP DRCOG

Lisa Hamzah MA MBBS MRCP

Ruth V Reed MA MBBChir MRCPCH

David Phillips MA MBBchir MRCP DipGUM DFFP

4th edition

Published by ISC Medical
97 Judd Street, London WC1H 9JG
www.iscmedical.co.uk - Tel: 0845 226 9487

4th edition: ISBN13: 978-1-905812-21-9
A catalogue record for this book is available from the British Library.

1st Edition: January 2006
2nd Edition: July 2006
3rd Edition: September 2007
This Edition: October 2011

Printed in the United Kingdom by:
Purbrooks Ltd, Gresham Way, Wimbledon Park, London SW19 8ED

The authors have, as far as possible, taken care to ensure that the information given in this text is accurate and up to date. However, readers are strongly advised to confirm that the information with regards to specific patient management complies with current legislation, guidelines and local protocols.

The information within this text is intended as a study aid for the purpose of the GPST/GPVTS selection examinations. It is not intended, nor should it be used as a medical reference for the direct management of patients or their conditions.

PREFACE & INSTRUCTIONS

Introduced in 2006, Extended Match Questions (EMQs) now form an integral part of Stage 2 of the assessment for entry into General Practice Specialist Training (GPST).

This book contains a wide range of practice questions which will help you revise and practice for the exam.

EMQs work on the following basis:

1 – You are offered a list of options from which you will need to pick the answers to the questions posed. There can be as many as 10 options.

2 – You are given a list of statements or questions. For each of them you must identify the best possible answer from the list of options given.

IMPORTANT NOTES

Unless explicitly mentioned in the question itself, each statement or question has a unique answer.

Each option can be used once, more than once, or not at all.

The exam is not negatively marked. You should therefore aim to attempt every single question to maximise your score. If you do not know the answer, first eliminate the options that you know to be incorrect and then pick one out of the remaining options.

Best of luck.

CONTENTS

Biology / Pathology

1 Cells of the immune system. **BIO/PATH**

Options
1 Neutrophils
2 Eosinophils
3 Basophils
4 Monocytes
5 B lymphocytes
6 T lymphocytes

Questions
Select the cell type that is most appropriate.

a. Are called osteoclasts in the bones when activated.

b. Mast cells are their equivalent in tissues.

c. In tissue, have the function of mediating type I hypersensitivity caused by interaction with antigen bound to IgE.

d. Have CD4 receptors.

e. Produce antibodies.

f. Active against multicellular parasitic organisms.

| 2 | Immunoglobulins | BIO/PATH |

Options
    1 IgG
    2 IgA
    3 IgM
    4 IgD
    5 IgE

Questions

Pick the most appropriate answer.

a. Predominantly produced by mucosa-associated lymphoid tissue.

b. Consists of a pentamer joined by a J chain.

c. Is involved in the primary immune response.

d. Is the most abundant in adult serum.

e. Rises in response to parasitic infections.

f. Is increased in atopic patients.

3 Hypersensitivity reactions   BIO/PATH

Options
1 Type I
2 Type II
3 Type III
4 Type IV

Questions
Which type of hypersensitivity reaction is involved?

a. Involves cell-mediated cytotoxic T cells.

b. Examples include the Mantoux test.

c. Transfusion reaction is an example.

d. Can lead to anaphylaxis in systemic disease.

e. The process is of circulating antibody that reacts with free antigen, forming immune complexes. These deposit, leading to complement activation with mast cell degranulation and increased neutrophil phagocytosis.

f. Haemolytic anaemia is an example.

g. Systemic lupus erythematosus is an example.

h. Extrinsic alveolitis is an example.

4 Types of transplant

BIO/PATH

Options
1 Autograft
2 Syngraft
3 Allograft
4 Xenograft

Questions
What type of transplant are these?

a. Transplant between non-identical individuals.

b. Transplant between individuals of different species.

c. Transplant between genetically identical individuals.

d. Transplant within one individual.

5 Autoantibodies   BIO/PATH

Options
1 Hashimoto's thyroiditis
2 Graves' disease
3 Addison's disease
4 Insulin-dependent diabetes mellitus
5 Myasthenia gravis
6 Lambert-Eaton myasthenic syndrome
7 Guillain-Barré syndrome
8 Goodpasture syndrome
9 Primary biliary cirrhosis
10 Autoimmune haemolytic anaemia

Questions
Which disease do antibodies to the following antigens cause?

a. Thyroid stimulating hormon receptor.

b. Islet cells.

c. Mitochondria.

d. Glomerular and lung basement membrane.

e. Glutamic acid decarboxylase.

f. Calcium channels on nerve endings.

g. Acetylcholine receptor.

h. Peripheral nerve myelin components.

6 Metabolic medicine   BIO/PATH

Options

1 Hypernatraemia
2 Hyponatraemia
3 Hypercalcaemia
4 Hypocalcaemia
5 Hyperkalaemia

Questions

What metabolic state can these cause?

a. Haemolysis.

b. Hyperosmolar non-ketotic state.

c. Liver cirrhosis.

d. Water overload.

e. Sarcoid.

f. Hypoparathyroidism.

7 Raised plasma enzymes   BIO/PATH

Options
1 Alkaline phosphatase (ALP)
2 Alanine aminotransferase (ALT)
3 Aspartate transaminase (AST)
4 Amylase
5 Creatinine Kinase (CK)
6 Gamma glutamyl transpeptidase (GGT)
7 Ferritin
8 Lactase dehydrogenase (LDH)

Questions
Which enzyme is most likely to be raised in these situations?

a. Thalassaemia.

b. Cholestasis.

c. Increased osteoblast activity in bone disease.

d. Pancreatitis.

e. Statin therapy.

f. Haemochromatosis.

8 Screening				BIO/PATH

Options

1 d/(b+c)
2 d/(b+d)
3 a/(a+b)
4 d/(a+c)
5 a/(a+c)
6 a/(a+d)
7 a/(a-d)
8 d/(b-c)

	True Positives	True Negatives
Test Positives	a	b
Test Negatives	c	d

Questions

Based on the table above, which expression represents the following statistical terms?

a. Sensitivity.

b. Specificity.

c. Positive predictive value.

B Cardiology

9 Cardiac investigations   CARDIO

Options
1 12-lead electrocardiogram
2 Bubble test
3 Chest X-ray
4 Coronary angiogram
5 Electrophysiological studies
6 Event recorder
7 Exercise tolerance test
8 Right heart catheterization
9 Tilt test
10 Transthoracic echocardiogram

Questions
Which of the investigations from the list above is best suited to the following situations

a. Detecting accessory conduction pathways.

b. Demonstrating the presence of a patent foramen ovale.

c. Confirming paroxysmal atrial fibrillation.

d. Revealing pericardial calcification.

e. Quantifying pulmunary hypertension.

f. Visualising a large pulmonary embolus.

10 Acute pulmonary oedema   CARDIO

Options
1 Diuretics
2 Oxygen
3 Nitrates
4 Morphine
5 Frusemide
6 Nitroprusside

Questions
Select the best option

a. Is not usually used to treat acute pulmonary oedema.

b. Is the first line treatment of acute pulmonary oedema.

c. Is usually given as 10 mg intravenously, in 2 mg aliquots.

d. Is usually given as 40-80 mg i.v.

e. Is titrated up every 10 minutes, until clinical improvement occurs or blood pressure falls to < 110 mmHg.

11 Consequences of heart disease.   CARDIO

Options
1 Ball and cage mechanical heart valve
2 Past bacterial endocarditis
3 Rheumatic heart disease
4 Pericarditis
5 Hypertrophic cardiomyopathy

Questions
Choose the most suitable statement.

a. Can be associated with acute renal failure.

b. Long term anticoagulation requires a target INR of 3.5.

c. May have been caused by poor dental hygiene.

d. St Vitus dance is a recognised feature.

e. This is a cause of sudden death in young people.

12 Murmurs   CARDIO

Options
1 Aortic regurgitation
2 Aortic stenosis
3 Mitral regurgitation
4 Pulmonary stenosis
5 Mitral stenosis
6 Pulmonary regurgitation
7 Congenital AV malformation

Questions
You examine a patient and discover a murmur. For each of the following additional features, identify the most likely murmur from the list above.

a. A collapsing pulse.

b. Angina and exertional syncope.

c. A pan-systolic murmur radiating to the axilla.

d. A low-pitched mid-diastolic murmur heard best when the patient is rolled onto their left side.

e. An ejection systolic murmur, heard loudest in the left sternal edge, radiating to the left shoulder.

13 Murmurs

CARDIO

Options
1. Pansystolic murmur
2. Splinter haemorrhages
3. A murmur sounds louder on inspiration
4. "Spider-like" fingers
5. Atrial fibrillation

Questions
Which of the clinical signs above best match the following statements?

a. A 26 year old patient presents with sudden onset tearing chest pain radiating through to the back.

b. Is consistent with right-sided valve defects.

c. A vegetation is found on a heart valve on echocardiography.

d. Is most likely to be caused by a mitral valve defect rather than any other valve abnormality.

e. Can be caused by mitral regurgitation or a ventricular septal defect.

14 Arrhythmias   CARDIO

Options
1. Agonal rhythm
2. Atrial fibrillation
3. Atrial flutter
4. Bradycardia
5. Mobitz type 1
6. Mobitz type 2
7. Supraventricular tachycardia
8. Torsade de pointes
9. Ventricular fibrillation
10. Ventricular tachycardia
11. Wolf-Parkinson-White

Questions
Which of the above cardiac rhythms best fits the descriptions given below?

a. Characterised by a regular saw-tooth pattern of 'p' waves.

b. A slow irregular rhythm seen towards the end of an unsuccessful cardiac arrest as the heart dies.

c. If asymptomatic, atropine is an appropriate treatment option.

d. Characterised by a progressive lengthening of the 'p-r' interval culminating in a 'p' wave with no accompanying 'qrs' complex.

e. Direct current cardioversion is the only treatment to be of likely benefit.

f. Is associated with long 'Q-T' syndromes and can be treated with intravenous magnesium.

15 The jugular venous pressure (JVP)   CARDIO

Options
1 Right heart failure
2 Tricuspid stenosis
3 Atrial fibrillation
4 Tricuspid regurgitation
5 Complete heart block

Questions
Which of the options above cause these changes to the JVP?

a. Absent a waves.

b. Large v waves.

c. Increase in all elements.

d. Cannon waves.

e. Large a waves.

16 Heart sounds   CARDIO

Options
1 First heart sound
2 Second heart sound
3 Third heart sound
4 Fourth heart sound

Questions
Which heart sound do these apply to?

a. Closure of the mitral valve.

b. Closure of the tricuspid valve.

c. Becomes loud in pulmonary hypertension.

d. Occurs in hyperdynamic states such as pregnancy.

e. Always pathological.

f. Splitting occurs in atrial septal defects.

g. Is soft in mitral stenosis.

17 Electrocardiogram (ECG) abnormalities CARDIO

Options
1 Left bundle branch block
2 Right bundle branch block
3 Right ventricle hypertrophy
4 Low voltage ECG
5 Short PR interval

Questions
Which ECG abnormality in the list above applies to each of the following?

a. Wolff-Parkinson-White syndrome leads to this.

b. RSR pattern in V1.

c. Wide QRS with an M pattern in V5.

d. May be seen in dextrocardia.

e. Pericardial effusion will cause this.

f. Cor pulmonale can lead to this.

18 ECG abnormalities   CARDIO

Options

1 Prolonged QT interval
2 ST depression
3 ST elevation
4 Persistent left bundle branch block
5 Pulseless electrical activity
6 Right bundle branch block
7 The "reverse tick" sign

Questions

Which ECG abnormality applies?

a. Can be caused by Digoxin therapy.

b. Can be caused by a posterior myocardial infarction.

c. Persistence of this sign may be an indication of a left ventricular aneurysm following a myocardial infarction.

d. Part of Romano-Ward syndrome.

e. Part of Jervell and Lange-Nielsen syndrome.

19 Arrhythmias   **CARDIO**

Options
1 Sinus tachycardia
2 Atrial fibrillation
3 Broad-complex tachycardia
4 Re-entrant tachycardia
5 Ventricular tachycardia

Questions
Pick the appropriate tachycardia,

a. Wolff-Parkinson-White syndrome is an example.

b. Anxiety will cause this.

c. P waves are absent.

d. There are capture beats, fusion beats and p waves are dissociated from the QRS complex.

e. Supraventricular tachycardia with bundle branch block is an example.

20 Valvular heart disease — CARDIO

Options
1 Mitral stenosis
2 Mitral regurgitation
3 Aortic stenosis
4 Aortic regurgitation
5 Tricuspid regurgitation

Questions
Which is the most likely diagnosis for the following statements?

a. Congenital bicuspid valve is a risk factor.

b. Giant v waves are seen in the JVP.

c. Classic signs include pistol-shot femoral pulses and positive Quincke's sign.

d. An early diastolic murmur on leaning forward in expiration at the left sternal edge.

e. A pulsatile liver may be detected.

| 21 | Congenital heart disease | CARDIO |

Options
1 Atrial septal defect
2 Ventricular septal defect
3 Patent ductus arteriosus
4 Tetralogy of Fallot
5 Coarctation of the aorta

Questions
Which condition is associated with each of the following?

a. Radiofemoral delay.

b. Association with berry aneurysms, Turner's syndrome and bicuspid aortic valve.

c. May be closed with indomethacin.

d. Maladie de Roger.

e. The three types are ostium secundum, ostium primum and sinus venosus.

22 Chest pain **CARDIO**

Options
1 Angina
2 Myocardial infarction
3 Anxiety
4 Dissecting aortic aneurysm
5 Pancreatitis
6 Pneumonia
7 Pericarditis
8 Pneumothorax
9 Pulmonary embolus (PE)
10 Tietze's syndrome

Questions
Pick the most likely diagnosis for the following presentations.

a. Severe boring chest pain with an amylase of 3000 (normal is below 200).

b. Central crushing chest pain occuring at rest. Three days later there is new shortness of breath which wakes the patient up at night and occurs on climbing stairs.

c. A patient with gross ascites due to an intra-abdominal carcinoma, develops chest pain and shortness of breath.

d. A tall thin young man who suddenly develops chest pains. His chest is hyper-resonant on percussion.

e. Sharp, constant sternal pain relieved by sitting forwards. This pain is worse on lying on the left side and on inspiration.

23 | Clinical signs of structural heart abnormalities   **CARDIO**

Options
1 Aortic stenosis
2 Aortic incompetence
3 Mitral stenosis
4 Tricuspid regurgitation
5 Hypertrophic cardiomyopathy
6 Atrial septal defect
7 Ventricular septal defect
8 Ebstein's anomaly
9 Mitral valve prolapse
10 Patent ductus arteriosus

Questions
Pick the most likely structural heart abnormality for these examination findings.

a. There is a harsh pan-systolic murmur, loudest at the lower left sternal edge and inaudible at the apex. The apex is not displaced.

b. There is a soft late systolic murmur at the apex, radiating to the axilla.

c. The pulse is slow rising and the apex is heaving in character.

d. The pulse is regular and jerky in character. The cardiac impulse is hyperdynamic and not displaced. There is a mid-systolic murmur, with no ejection click, loudest at the left sternal edge.

e. There is a constant 'machinery-like' murmur throughout systole and disastole. The patient is clubbed and cyanosed.

C   Dermatology

24 | Rosacea | DERM

Options
1 Telangiectasia
2 Rhinophyma
3 Lymphoedema
4 Pyoderma faciale
5 Pilosebaceous follicles
6 Demodex folliculorum

Questions
Concerning long-term cutaneous complications of chronic rosacea, match the descriptions with their name.

a. A craggy bulbous enlargement of the nose.

b. Visible superficial sprays of dilated blood vessels.

c. May be called rosacea fulminans.

d. Phymomatous swellings of the face causing chronic inflammation and tissue oedema leading to thickening of the soft tissues and prominence of the pilosebaceous openings.

25 Systemic treatment of rosacea   DERM

Options

1 Isotretinoin
2 Dapsone
3 Antimalarials
4 Clonidine
5 Beta-blockers
6 Mirtazapine

Questions

Pick the drug that is being described.

a. Controls flushing and acts as a presynaptic alpha 2 antagonist.

b. Contra-indicated in asthma.

c. Licensed for use in leprosy.

d. Hydroxychloroquine is an example.

e. Is a vitamin A analogue.

f. Is a centrally acting alpha blocker.

26 Differential diagnosis of acne vulgaris — DERM

Options
1. Rosacea
2. Acne agminata
3. Acne necrotica
4. Acne keloid
5. Comedo naevus
6. Epidermoid cysts
7. Milia
8. Perioral dermatitis
9. Pityrosporum folliculitis
10. Seborrhoeic dermatitis

Questions
Which conditions best fit the descriptions below:

a. This is a scaly erythematous rash which can occur on the face, chest and scalp. It frequently affects the nasolabial folds and ears. Petaloid lesions may be found over the sternum.

b. Found in young adults and teenagers. It is associated with exposure to the sun. There are multiple tiny, itchy papules and pustules on the shoulders and back. There are no comedones and the condition responds to topical imidazoles.

c. These have a punctum from which cheesy material may be expelled.

d. The most common differential diagnosis of acne vulgaris.

e. Young females may develop papules and pustules around the lips, sometimes resulting from inappropriate use of topical steroids.

27   Complications of acne   DERM

Options
1 Pyoderma faciale
2 Acne excoriee
3 Post-inflammatory hyperpigmentation
4 Gram-negative folliculitis
5 Acne conglobata
6 Acne fulminans

Questions
Select the complication of acne being described.

a. More commonly occurs in Afro-Caribbean patients. Treatment can be attempted with topical azelaic but prevention with early effective acne treatments is better.

b. Occurs in young females. It results from repeated picking and resembles prurigo.

c. Proteus is often implicated and may result from long-term antibiotic treatment.

d. A severe form of acne presenting with large nodules, abscesses and sinuses. There is suppuration and scarring. It is associated with hidradenitis suppurativa.

e. In this form there is an immune reaction to Propionibacterium acnes.

28 Eczema - treatments   DERM

Options
1 Dietary modifications
2 Emollients
3 Topical steroids
4 Antihistamines
5 Chinese herbal remedies

Questions
Pick the most likely treatment being described.

a. Hepatitis is a known side effect. This treatment is of little use in weepy eczema.

b. Can make the patient drowsy.

c. If there is no improvement after 2 months this therapy should be abandoned.

d. Potent preparations should be avoided on the face.

e. Palms and soles may require super-potent forms.

29 Terminology   DERM

Options
1 Alopecia
2 Crust
3 Erosion
4 Fissure
5 Induration
6 Macule
7 Papule
8 Plaque
9 Vesicle
10 Wheal

Questions
Match up these terms and descriptions.

a. A solid well circumscribed bump rising from the skin. It is usually under 1cm across.

b. Hair loss.

c. Crack.

d. Flat, well defined area of changed skin pigmentation.

e. An area of localised hardening of soft tissue.

f. A raised itchy lesion often associated with allergy.

30 Skin and systemic disease   DERM

Options
1 Diabetes mellitus
2 Coeliac disease
3 Inflammatory bowel disease
4 Rheumatoid arthritis
5 Systemic lupus erythematosus
6 Neoplasia
7 Lyme disease
8 Cutaneous vasculitis
9 Graves' disease

Questions
For each of the following skin conditions, match the most appropriate disease above.

a. Acanthosis nigricans.

b. Necrobiosis lipoidica.

c. Erythema nodosum.

d. Pre-tibial myxoedema.

e. Erythema chronicum migrans.

f. Dermatitis herpetiformis.

31 Serious skin conditions   DERM

Options
1   Melanoma
2   Kaposi's sarcoma
3   Leprosy
4   Syphilis
5   Basal cell carcinoma
6   Actinic keratosis
7   Mycosis fungoides
8   Bowen's disease
9   Paget's disease of the nipple
10   Metastatic cancer

Questions
What is the most likely skin condition?

a.   Human herpes virus 8 is implicated.

b.   Cutaneous T-cell lymphoma usually of CD4 type.

c.   Slowly growing red scaly plaque, often found on the lower legs. Histology show full-thickness dysplasia. Infrequently progresses to squamous cell carcinoma.

d.   Cutaneous sign of intraductal breast cancer.

e.   Occurs on sun-exposed areas, appearing as crumbly yellow-white crusts.

32 Different types of eczema   DERM

Options
1. Irritant contact
2. Allergic contact
3. Photodermatitis
4. Atopic
5. Adult seborrhoeic eczema
6. Discoid
7. Asteatotic
8. Lichen simplex
9. Juvenile plantar dermatosis
10. Infantile seborrhoeic eczema

Questions
What is the most likely type of eczema being described?

a. Asthma and hayfever are associated with this condition.

b. Agents containing nickel are often implicated.

c. Pityrosporum yeasts plays a part in the pathophysiology.

d. Presents as discrete coin-shaped patches on the trunk and limbs.

e. Cases usually present before 12 weeks of age.

33 | Differential diagnosis of psoriasis | DERM

Options
1 Lichen planus
2 Pityriasis rosea
3 Pityriasis rubra pilaris
4 Urticaria
5 Drug eruptions
6 Seborrhoeic eczema
7 Discoid eczema

Questions
Match the most likely skin condition to each of the statements below.

a. Lesions tend to be transient and very itchy.

b. Has the feature of islands of 'normal' skin.

c. Initially features a herald patch.

d. Lesions are violaceous, flat-topped and polygonal

e. Wickham's striae are a feature.

34 Skin neoplasia   DERM

Options
1 Seborrrhoeic warts
2 Dermatofibromas
3 Banal naevi
4 Angiomas
5 Basal cell carcinomas
6 Actinic keratoses
7 Squamous cell carcinomas
8 Melanomas

Questions
Match the most likely skin condition to each of the statements below.

a. Caused by benign overgrowth of blood vessels.

b. Caused by chronic solar damage and found on bald heads of elderly patients.

c. Are the most common type of skin cancer in post-transplant patients.

d. May be non-pigmented.

e. Have a 'stuck on' appearance.

35 | Malignant melanoma   DERM

Options
1 Lentigo maligna
2 Nodular
3 Acral
4 Amelanocytic
5 Rodent ulcer

Questions
Which type of melanoma is being described in each of the cases below?

a. Most commonly found in those of dark-skinned races.

b. Most commonly on the trunk, upper arms and thighs.

c. Most commonly found on the palms of the hands and the soles of the feet.

d. Commonly found as a small asymmetric pigmented patch. As it grows within a regular border, it tends to remain on the surface before it eventually penetrates to deeper levels.

e. This lesion has a short "flat phase" and often ulcerates.

f. This is seen as a non-pigmented lesion.

36 Rashes   DERM

Options
1 Plaque psoriasis
2 Guttate psoriasis
3 Pityriasis versicolor
4 Actinic keratosis
5 Mycoses fungoides
6 Paget's disease
7 Lupus vulgaris
8 Pityriasis lichenoides
9 Tinea cruris

Questions
Pick the most suitable answer.

a. Flat finely scaled hyper-pigmented lesions which typically leave hypo-pigmentation upon resolution after skin tanning.

b. A skin manifestation of tuberculosis.

c. Described as silvery scaly or salmon pink lesions topped with silvery scales most commonly found on extensor surfaces.

d. Often described as a shower of small erythematous lesions.

e. By definition, these lesions are found in skin creases e.g. submammary or groin regions.

37 Investigations

Options
1 Bacterial swab
2 Viral swab
3 Wood's light
4 Patch testing
5 Skin prick test
6 Punch biopsy
7 Serology
8 Doppler ultrasound scanner
9 Cryotherapy
10 Electron microscopy

Questions
Pick the most appropriate investigation to diagnose the conditions below.

a. Tinea capitis.

b. Cold sores.

c. Molluscum contagiosum (MC).

d. Type 4 hypersensitivity.

e. Lichen sclerosis.

38 Formulations   DERM

Options
1 Soaks
2 Shampoos
3 Lotions
4 Paints
5 Gels
6 Creams
7 Ointments
8 Powders
9 Pastes

Questions
Pick the most likely formulation being described.

a. Transparent semi-solid emulsions which tend to become a liquid on contact with a warm surface.

b. Liquid formulations, either in water or alcohol. They can have a cooling effect, which can be useful on acutely inflamed areas.

c. Hydrate the skin. They spread fairly easily and tend to be more accepted cosmetically. They can be used for the face, flexures and palms.

d. Crystals are disolved in water to produce a solution.

e. Greasy and form an occlusive layer. They are good for chronic conditions. Soft paraffin is used as an ingredient.

39 Potency of steroids   DERM

Options
1 Mild
2 Moderate
3 Potent
4 Very potent

Questions
What term best describes these steroids' potency?

a. Clobetasone butyrate 0.05%.

b. Mometasone furoate 0.1%.

c. Hydrocortisone 2.5%.

d. Hydrocortisone 0.1%.

e. Betamethasone valerate 0.1%.

f. Clobetasol proprionate 0.05%.

40 Hair loss   **DERM**

Options
1 Alopecia areata.
2 Diffuse alopecia
3 Androgenetic alopecia
4 Non-scarring alopecia
5 Scarring alopecia
6 Alopecia totalis
7 Trichotillomania
8 Telogen effluvium

Questions
Match the most likely description to the type of hair loss.

a. Increased shedding, often post-natal.

b. Localised hair loss.

c. Irregular patch or patches of scalp or eyebrow epilation with residual short hairs.

d. A consequence of lichen planus.

e. A complication of iron deficiency, anaemia or hypothyroidism.

41 Scaly rashes on trunk   DERM

Options
1 Plaque psoriasis
2 Guttate psoriasis
3 Lichen planus
4 Pityriasis rosea
5 Pityriasis lichenoides
6 Tinea corporis
7 Persistent superficial dermatitis
8 Mycosis fungoides

Questions
Which rash matches each of the following descriptions?

a. Very itchy flat-topped violaceous papules.

b. Scaly areas with raised edges and central clearing.

c. Silvery scaly plaques with a well-defined edge.

d Herald patch with multiple oval pink patches.

42 Drugs in dermatology   DERM

Options
1 Oral steroids
2 Urea compounds
3 Salicylates
4 Antihistamines
5 Vitamin D derivatives
6 Vitamin A derivatives
7 Dithranol compounds
8 Tar preparations
9 Methotrexate preparations
10 Oral retinoids

Questions
Pick the most likely drug for each of the following statements.

a. These are highly teratogenic; side effects include hair loss, nose bleeds, sore lips and dryness of mucous membranes.

b. Risks with this drug include bone marrow suppression and hepatic fibrosis.

c. This is a synthetic derivative of chrysarobin, which comes from the araroba tree.

d. Calcipotriol is an example.

e. Causes reduction of scale by destruction of keratin.

43 Psychogenic skin conditions   DERM

Options
1. Habit tick nail dystrophy
2. Nail biting
3. Neurotic excoriations
4. Lip licking
5. Hair pulling habit
6. Excoriated acne
7. Formication
8. Dermatitis artefacta
9. Dermatological pathomimicry
10. Habituation to dressings

Questions
Match the most likely condition:

a. A noted feature in alcohol withdrawal.

b. Deliberate aggravation of skin conditions.

c. Short nails with a ragged free edge are a clinical sign.

d. The patient intends to deceive in order to gain attention or another secondary gain.

e. An unconscious habit of rubbing the cuticles leads to a ladder pattern of transverse ridges and furrows running up the centre of a thumbnail.

44 Urticaria subtypes	DERM

Options
1 Aquagenic
2 Cholinergic
3 Cold
4 Delayed pressure
5 Immediate pressure
6 Localised heat
7 Vibratory angio-oedema
8 Solar

Questions
Which subtype of urticaria is associated with the following features?

a. Will exhibit dermographism.

b. Induced by the use of power tools.

c. Lesions appear after 4-6 hours of pressure.

d. More commonly presents in the peripheries.

e. A response to anxiety, heat, exertion. Anticholinergics may help.

45 Types of ulcer   **DERM**

Options
1. Large vessel arterial disease
2. Mixed arterial and venous
3. Small vessel disease
4. Sloughing
5. Haematological
6. Rodent ulcer
7. Neuropathic ulcer
8. Infective
9. Atrophie blanche
10. Venous

Questions
Match the best type of ulcer

a. Patients with rheumatoid arthritis, diabetes and systemic sclerosis get this type.

b. Has a rolled edge or a heaped-up ulcer base and there is a failure to heal despite treatment.

c. Is punched out, deep and has a pale ulcer bed. There may also be surrounding hairloss.

d. Has a viscous yellow layer that is highly adherent to the wound.

e. Can be treated with multiple layer compression bandaging.

f. Will classically occur at pressure points.

46 Trade Names | DERM

Options

1 Modrasone ®
2 Diprosone ®
3 Diprosalic ®
4 Lotriderm ®
5 Betnovate N ®
6 Fucibet ®
7 Betnovate ®
8 Dermovate ®
9 Eumovate ®
10 Stiedex ®

Questions

What is the trade name for these drugs?

a. Betamethasone dipropionate.

b. Betamethasone valerate.

c. Betamethasone valerate + neomycin.

d. Clobetasone butyrate.

e. Clobetasol propionate.

47 Pigmentation in systemic disease   DERM

Options
1 Tuberous sclerosis
2 Albininism
3 Neurofibromatosis
4 Addison's disease
5 Myxoedema
6 Alpha 1 antitrypsin deficiency

Questions
Match the pigmentation pattern to the most likely disease.

a. Axillary and inguinal freckles.

b. Generalised hyperpigmentation.

c. Ash-leaf hypopigmented macules.

d. Generalised hypopigmentation.

D Endocrinology

48 Symptoms in endocrinology — ENDO

Options
1 Addison's disease
2 Hyperthyroidism
3 Primary hypothyroidism
4 Phaeochromocytoma
5 Cushing's disease
6 Acromegaly
7 Craniopharyngioma

Questions
Which of the options above is the most likely cause for each of the symptoms below?

a. Postural hypotension.

b. Osteoporosis in pre-menopausal women.

c. Secondary amenorrhoea, visual disturbance and galactorrhoea.

d. Impaired glucose tolerance.

e. Sweaty palms and headache.

49 The reproductive axis ENDO

Options
1 Primary hypogonadism
2 Cushing's disease
3 Hypogonadotrophic hypogonadism
4 Kallman's syndrome
5 Sheehan's syndrome
6 Neuroleptic therapy

Questions
Choose the best response

a. Acquired failure of hormone secretion due to infarction of the pituitary gland.

b. Another term for testicular failure in a man.

c. Surgery may be a treatment option for this cause of hormonal disease.

d. Galactorrhoea is a known complication.

e. A failure in the reproductive axis associated with anosmia.

| 50 | Diabetic drugs | | ENDO |

Options
1 Biguanide
2 Alpha-glucosidase inhibitors
3 Sulphonylureas
4 Thiazolidinediones

Questions
Choose the most likely oral hypoglycaemic agent for each of the following statements.

a. The main side effect is flatulence.

b. Rosiglitazone is an example.

c. Metformin is an example.

d. Slows absorption of carbohydrate.

e. Increases insulin secretion.

f. Reduces glucose absorption from the gut and increases insulin sensitivity.

g. Gliclazide is an example.

51 Diabetic emergencies ENDO

Options
1 Diabetic ketoacidosis
2 Hyperosmolar non-ketotic state
3 Hypoglycaemia

Questions
Which is the best option for each of the following situations?

a. Does not occur in Type 1 diabetes.

b. Accurate timing of short-acting insulin can avoid this consequence in a patient who is socialising.

c. Administering treatment via the buccal mucosa is useful.

d. Most likely to give rise to seizures.

e. Can occur in Addisonian crisis.

52 Pituitary problems   ENDO

Options
1 Hypopituitarism
2 Pituitary adenoma
3 Pituitary apoplexy
4 Craniopharyngioma
5 Hyperprolactinaemia
6 Acromegaly
7 Diabetes insipidus
8 Syndrome of inappropriate anti-diuretic hormon (SIADH)

Questions
Which is the most likely pituitary problem?

a. Can be chromophobic.

b. Originates from Rathke's pouch.

c. Is the most common pituitary disorder.

d. Could be nephrogenic or cranial.

e. Due to growth hormone secreting pituitary tumour.

Ear, Nose & Throat

53 Hearing loss   ENT

Options
1 Ear wax
2 Otitis media
3 Barotrauma
4 Previous ear operation
5 Trauma
6 Drugs
7 Mumps
8 Idiopathic

Questions
Which is the most likely cause of hearing loss in these scenarios?

a. A cause of neuritis affecting the VIII nerve in children.

b. Divers are at risk from this.

c. By far the commonest cause of deafness.

d. Often self-limiting, associated with a viral illness.

54 Hearing aids   ENT

Options
  1 Behind-the-ear
  2 In-the-ear and canal
  3 Body
  4 Bone conduction
  5 Cochlear implant

Questions
Pick the most likely hearing aid type.

a. Necessary when there is bilateral ear canal atresia.

b. The most expensive type.

c. The most commonly used type by the National Health Service.

d. Sound is converted in an external processor into electrical signals which are then fed into a secondary device.

55 Causes of disequilibrium ENT

Options
1 Vestibular neuronitis
2 Acute otitis media
3 Chronic otitis media
4 Positional vertigo
5 Acoustic neuroma
6 Ménière's disease
7 Ageing
8 Transient ischaemic attacks
9 Vertebrobasilar ischaemia
10 Epileptic fits

Questions
In each of the following, which is the cause of disequilibrium?

a. Characterised by sudden, relatively short episodes of vertigo which can be brought on when getting out of bed.

b. This involves episodic vertigo and fluctuating sensorineural hearing impairment which is usually accompanied by tinnitus and fullness of the ear(s).

c. The pathological process is that of endolymphatic hydrops.

d. These attacks can be triggered when someone reaches up to perform an activity e.g hanging washing on a line or retrieving an object from a top shelf.

e. Has a typical presentation of acute vertigo which can take several days to settle. There are no other neurological symptoms and in particular no hearing loss or tinnitus.

56 Painful mouth   ENT

Options

1. Aphthous ulcer
2. Traumatic ulcer
3. Candida
4. Herpetic ulcer
5. Fibrous traumatic polyp
6. Leukoplakia
7. Erythroplakia

Questions

What is the most likely cause of the pain in the mouth?

a. Removal of a white membrane reveals a raw mucosal area.

b. This is a raised white area on the inside of the cheek or on the tongue, associated with Epstein-Barr virus (EBV).

c. The presence of red raw raised areas which are related to trauma. Many are carcinoma in situ.

d. These can occur with poorly fitted dentures.

e. These regularly occur on mobile parts of the mucosa, such as the cheek and labiogingival sulci. Treatment includes topical antiseptics.

57 Stridor   ENT

Options
1. Laryngomalacia
2. Congenital abnormalities
3. Laryngotracheobronchitis
4. Acute epiglottitis
5. Bezoar
6. Laryngeal papillomatosis
7. Laryngeal trauma
8. Laryngeal neoplasia

Questions
Which is the most likely cause of stridor being discussed?

a. This is a potentially life-threatening condition.

b. The Heimlich manoeuvre may help.

c. An example is an anterior web between the true cords.

d. Due to soft cartilage the negative pressure of inspiration causes the trachea to collapse.

e. Haemophilus influenzae is responsible for this condition.

58 Neck lumps   ENT

Options
1 Thyroglossal cyst
2 Thyroid adenocarcinoma
3 Salivary calculus
4 Hashimoto's disease
5 Multinodular goitre
6 Thyroid nodule
7 Dermoid cysts
8 Lipomas
9 Lymph nodes
10 Sebaceous cysts

Questions
Associate the most appropriate neck lump to each of the following statements.

a. The lump will move on protraction of the tongue.

b. A painful swelling below or at the angle of the jaw, made worse at or before eating.

c. If these are enlarged in the neck, a diagnosis of neoplasm must be excluded.

d. A high uptake of isotope on nuclear medicine scans may result when investigating this condition.

e. These are multiple congenital anomalies occurring in the midline.

59 Definitions in ENT   **ENT**

Options
1 Tragus
2 Cacosmia
3 Cageusia
4 Cholesteatoma
5 Globus syndrome
6 Glottis
7 Antitragus
8 Ozaena
9 Quinsy
10 Rannula

Questions
Which of the above terms apply to the definitions below.

a. The true vocal cords.

b. An collection of squamous epithelial debris which can erode through the middle ear.

c. An area of cartilage anterior to the external auditory meatus on the external ear.

d. A sensation of a lump in the throat without true dysphagia.

e. An abscess above the tonsil.

60 The external ear   ENT

Options
1 Pre-auricular sinuses
2 Accessory auricles
3 Ramsay Hunt syndrome
4 Microtia
5 Perichondritis
6 Keratosis obturans
7 Furunculosis
8 Otomycosis
9 Exostosis
10 Tumours

Questions
Which external ear condition is being described in each of the following statements?

a. Herpes virus is implicated.

b. Inflammation of the covering of the cartilage.

c. The pinna consists of only a few skin tags.

d. Results from the anomalous tubercle growth of the branchial arches.

e. A bony outgrowth from the wall of the external auditory meatus.

61 Rhinitis

Options
1 Acute rhinitis
2 Purulent rhinitis
3 Membranous rhinitis
4 Diphtheria rhinitis
5 Syphilitic rhinitis
6 Rhinosporidiosis
7 Klebsiella rhinitis
8 Tuberculous rhinitis

Questions
Which types of rhinitis are being described below?

a. Fleshy nasal polyps often with grey specks upon them, which gives rise to a 'ripe strawberry appearance', caused by a yeast-like organism.

b. Rhinoscleroma is a term for this type of rhinitis.

c. 'Apple-jelly' nodules that characterise the skin condition can be demonstrated if the skin is pressed with a glass slide (diascopy).

d. A common cause of coryzal symptoms.

e. It is endemic only in India and Sri Lanka.

62 Pharyngeal anatomy   ENT

Options
1 Nasopharynx
2 Oropharynx
3 Valleculae
4 Tonsils
5 Soft palate
6 Larynx

Questions

Which option above best fits the statements below?

a. The posterior and lateral margins are formed by the pharyngeal constrictor muscles.

b. Lies between the tongue base and epiglottis and is a common site for fish bone foreign bodies

c. The posterior wall of this structure arches forward into the roof, which is formed by the basisphenoid. At the junction of the roof and posterior wall are situated the adenoids.

d. Extends from the posterior choanae to the soft palate.

e. The orifices of the Eustachian tubes are located here.

63 Laryngeal conditions   ENT

Options
1 Contact ulcer
2 Singer's node
3 Intubation granuloma
4 Vocal polyp
5 Reinke's oedema
6 Sensory dysfunction of the larynx
7 Laryngeal spasm
8 Vocal fold paralysis

Questions
Derive the most likely condition being described by each of the following statements.

a. Increased volume of contents in the subepithelial space beneath the vocal cords.

b. Appears as a smooth glistening body attached to one cord.

c. Arytenoid fixation would cause this.

d. Also called vocal nodules.

e. Found at the area of maximum vibration of the vocal cords, namely at the junction of the anterior third and posterior two-thirds of the cord.

64 Facial trauma   ENT

Options
1 Mandibular fracture
2 Malar fracture
3 Maxillary fracture
4 Orbital blow-out fracture
5 Nasal fracture

Questions
Which type of fracture best fits each of the following descriptions?

a. Le Fort described three different types.

b. This can result in extrusion of orbital contents into the maxillary antrum.

c. Palpation of the bony contours will reveal a step over the infraorbital ridge.

d. Management involves surgical correction by elevation of the depressed fragment via an incision in the temporal area.

e. The weakest part of this bone is the condylar neck.

65 Complications of facial trauma   ENT

Options
1 Respiratory obstruction
2 Haemorrhage
3 Inhalation injury
4 Cerebrospinal fluid rhinorrhoea
5 Cavernous sinus thrombosis
6 Septal haematoma
7 Fractured skull

Questions
Identify the complications that are described in each of the following statements.

a. Clear watery nasal discharge after facial injury makes you suspicious of this.

b. Can be caused by a retrograde infection via the facial veins.

c. Tracheostomy may be indicated to save life.

d. Can lead to ophthalmoplegia.

e. This is to be suspected is the patient develops a "panda eye" appearance.

| 66 | Headache and neck pain | ENT |

Options
1 Tension
2 Migraine
3 Cluster
4 Temporal arteritis
5 Trigeminal neuralgia
6 Post herpetic neuralgia
7 Sluder's or anterior ethmoidal neuralgia

Questions
Choose the most likely cause of the pain associated with each of the
following statements.

a. C-reactive protein (CRP) is useful to monitor this condition.

b. The sufferer typically experiences nasal stuffiness.

c. Ergot preparations are older medications that can help this condition.

d. This is the most common cause of a headache.

e. This is due to irritation of the nerve as it enters the roof of the nose.
   Severe pain originates from the roof of the nose and radiates to the
   forehead.

f. Is often described as a band-like pain around the head.

67 Oral cavity ENT

Options
1 Cleft palate
2 Lichen planus
3 Candida
4 Leukoplakia
5 Geographical tongue
6 Median rhomboid glossitis
7 Pellagra
8 Scurvy
9 Scarlet fever
10 Fordyce spots

Questions
Which disease of the mouth do the following statements refer to?

a. The lips are smooth and red; there is painful glossitis and dementia may develop.

b. There may be hallitosis and bleeding of the gums.

c. Small yellow papules can be seen on the buccal mucosa.

d. This is also called erythema migrans linguae.

e. Up to 5% of lesions in this condition may become malignant.

Gastroenterology

68 Abdominal pain | GASTRO

Options
1 Mesenteric adenitis
2 Inflammatory bowel disease
3 Acute appendicitis
4 Henoch-Schonlein purpura
5 Urinary tract infection
6 Constipation
7 Intussusception
8 Peptic ulcer
9 Renal stones
10 Bowel obstruction

Questions
Pick the most likely diagnosis for each of the following scenarios.

a. An 8 year old boy has lost his appetite and had central abdominal pain which has now radiated to the right iliac fossa.

b. A child complains of abdominal pain and has a purpuric rash on the buttocks with some joint pains.

c. A 4 month old girl has a recent episode of gastroenteritis. Now she has episodic screaming and pallor. There is some passage of blood and mucous in the stool. Ultrasound shows a 'doughnut sign'.

d. A 15 year old boy has had pains most nights for at least a month. He is afebrile. The pains are eased by drinking milk.

e. The patient has recurrent abdominal pain and malabsorption.

69 Histology of inflammatory bowel disease **GASTRO**

Options
1 'Cobblestone appearance'
2 'Skip lesion'
3 Granuloma
4 Angular stomatitis
5 Perianal skin tag
6 Fistula
7 Proctitis
8 Pseudopolyp

Questions
Choose the options that best match each of the following statements.

a. This is more common in ulcerative colitis than Crohn's disease

b. This is caused by deep linear ulcers within the mucosa.

c. This may lead to recurrent urinary infections and pneumaturia.

d. This contains mostly epithelioid histiocytes with scattered lymphocytes.

70 Oesophagus   GASTRO

Options
1 Sliding hiatus hernia
2 Paraoesophageal or rolling hiatus hernia
3 Carcinoma of the oesophagus
4 Achlasia
5 Strictures
6 Perforation

Questions
Pick the best option regarding the oesophagus.

a. Clinical features are acute severe pain in the chest, neck or upper abdomen with cervical crepitus and subcutaneous emphysema.

b. All or part of the stomach herniates through the oesophageal hiatus adjacent to the gastro-oesophageal junction, which remains in its normal anatomical position.

c. Dysphagia without weight loss is the cardinal symptom.

d. A hydropneumothorax on a chest radiograph is noted.

e. Due to idiopathic degeneration of the ganglion cells of Auerbach's myenteric plexus.

71 Malabsorption GASTRO

Options
1 Biliary insufficiency
2 Pancreatic insufficiency
3 Small bowel malabsorption
4 Bacterial overgrowth
5 Disruption of gut transport mechanism
6 Rapid bowel transit

Questions
By what mechanism do these disorders lead to malabsorption?

a. Cystic fibrosis.

b. Giardiasis.

c. Diphyllobothriasis.

d. Pseudomembranous colitis

e. Primary sclerosing cholangitis.

f. Post-vagotomy.

g. Post-operative blind loops.

72 Constipation — GASTRO

Options
1 Bulking agents
2 Faecal softeners
3 Osmotic laxatives
4 Stimulant laxatives

Questions
Pick the most appropriate class of medication.

a. These draw fluid into the bowel.

b. Senna is an example.

c. Sodium docusate is an example.

d. Glycerine suppository is an example.

e. These are polysaccharide polymers that act by retaining water in the gut lumen, softening the faeces and promoting peristalsis.

73 Causes of constipation   GASTRO

Options
1 Poor fibre intake
2 Hypothyroidism
3 Irritable bowel syndrome
4 Hypercalcaemia
5 Anal fissure
6 Carcinoma of the rectum
7 Carcinoma of the colon
8 Bowel obstruction
9 Pregnancy
10 Bed rest

Questions
What is the most likely cause of constipation in the following scenarios?

a. A 40 year old woman presents with a three-day history of constipation, colicky abdominal pain, distension and vomiting. She has not even passed wind. Bowel sounds are high pitched.

b. A 30 year old man complains of constipation and pain on defaecation. He also notices small amounts of fresh blood on the paper afterwards. He is unable to tolerate a rectal examination due to pain.

c. A 21 year old woman with mild learning difficulties complains of recent onset of abdominal distension, constipation, indigestion and amenorrhoea.

d. A 65 year old man complains of constipation, low mood, low back pain that prevents him from sleeping, fatigue and thirst.

74 Causes of dysphagia   GASTRO

Options
1   Achalasia
2   Bronchial carcinoma
3   Carcinoma of the oesophagus
4   Chronic benign stricture
5   Left atrial hypertrophy
6   Myasthenia gravis
7   Oesophageal candidiasis
8   Pharyngeal pouch
9   Plummer-Vinson syndrome
10 Reflux oesophagitis

Questions
What is the most likely diagnosis in the following scenarios?

a. A 50 year old obese woman complains of a burning retrosternal discomfort after eating and on lying down. She has also noticed excessive salivation and wheezing when supine.

b. A 35 year old housewife has noticed progressively worsening difficulty swallowing over several years. She has been troubled by regurgitation of undigested food and halitosis.

c. A 45 year old pale woman complains that food is sticking in the back of her throat. On examination she is found to have spoon shaped nails and a smooth tongue.

d. A 65 year old man complains of difficulty in swallowing. He finds that the first mouthful of food is easy to swallow but thereafter he has increasing difficulty in swallowing until he regurgitates undigested food. You notice a neck swelling on examination.

75 Colonic disorders   GASTRO

Options
1 Carcinoma of the caecum
2 Carcinoma of the sigmoid colon
3 Colonic polyp
4 Diverticulitis
5 Haemorrhoids
6 Irritable bowel syndrome
7 Sigmoid volvulus
8 Ulcerative colitis

Questions
What is the most likely diagnosis?

a. A 72 year old man presents with increasing tiredness over a one year period. He has a microcytic anaemia and a mass in the right iliac fossa.

b. A 33 year old woman consults you regarding symptoms of alternating diarrhoea and constipation associated with cramp like abdominal pain relieved on defecation.

c. A 76 year old man presents with weight loss, pain on eating and abdominal distension. Plain abdominal X-ray films show the so called 'coffee bean' sign.

d. An 82 year old woman presents to casualty with a distended abdomen. A plain adominal X-ray film shows gross faecal loading in the colon and gas in the small bowel. The rectum is empty.

e. A 39 year old woman complains of passing blood stained motions with mucus up to five times a day. Symptoms have persisted for over a month and are associated with weight loss. Symptoms worsened since she stopped smoking. Barium enema suggests a granular mucosa.

76 Biliary tract   GASTRO

Options
1 An acutely raised amylase
2 Percutaneous transhepatic cholangiography
3 Endoscopic retrograde cholangio-pancreatography
4 Persistently elevated amylase
5 Conjugated hyperbilirubinaemia
6 Unconjugated hyperbilirubinaemia
7 None of the above

Questions
For each of the following assertions, what is the most likely option?

a. May be due to Gilbert's syndrome.

b. Is associated with pseudocyst formation.

c. Frequently caused by stone in the common bile duct.

d. A prognostic marker in acute pancreatitis.

e. May cause pancreatitis.

G Haematology

| 77 Haematological neoplasia | HAEM |

Options
1. Acute lymphoblastic leukaemia (ALL)
2. Acute myeloid leukaemia (AML)
3. Chronic myeloid leukaemia (CML)
4. Chronic lymphocytic leukaemia (CLL)
5. Hodgkin's lymphoma
6. Non-Hodgkin's lymphoma
7. Myeloma

Questions
Pick the most likely condition for the following:

a. Characterised by Reed-Sternberg cells.

b. Philadelphia chromosome seen in 90% of patients.

c. Auer rods are common.

d. Bence Jones protein is detected in urine

e. Lymphoblasts in blood and marrow.

f. 20% produce light chains.

g. It is often picked up as an incidental finding in the elderly.

h. Polycythaemia vera and CML can convert to this.

78 Coagulation disorders   HAEM

Options
1 Haemophilia A
2 Haemophilia B
3 Von Willebrand's disease
4 Disseminated intravascular coagulation

Questions
Pick the most likely disease

a. Autosomal dominant condition.

b. Commonest inherited coagulopathy in the UK.

c. Deficiency of factor VIII.

d. Also known as Christmas disease.

e. Deficiency of factor IX.

79 | Interpretation of haematological results | HAEM

Options
1 Beta thalassaemia minor
2 Cytotoxic drugs
3 Rheumatoid arthritis
4 Alcoholic arthritis
5 Idiopathic thrombocytopaenic purpura
6 Myelodysplasia
7 Folate deficiency
8 Acute myeloid leukaemia
9 Chronic myeloid leukaemia
10 Chronic lymphocytic leukaemia

Questions
Choose the most likely diagnosis

a. A 50 year old woman with an Hb 9.0, MCV 87, WCC 8.1, platelets 450, serum ferritin 300.

b. A 50 year old man with long standing epilepsy, Hb 10.1, MCV 115, WCC 3.8, platelets 243.

c. 21 year old woman, on a booking visit to antenatal clinic has Hb 9.7, MCV 71, MCH 27, red cell count, 6.7, WCC 6.4, platelets 310, HbA_2 >3.5%.

d. A 75 year old woman being investigated for fatigue. Hb 8.9, MCV 102, WCC 4.5, platelets 160.

Note:
Hb = Haemoglobin
MCV = Mean corpuscular volume
WCC = White cell count
MCH = Mean corpuscular haemoglobin
HbA_2 = Haemoglobin alpha 2

Infectious Diseases

80 HIV/AIDS   ID

Options
1 Pneumocystis carinii pneumonia (PCP)
2 Mycobacterium tuberculosis
3 Streptococcus
4 Human herpes virus 8
5 Epstein Barr virus (EBV)
6 Cytomegalovirus (CMV)
7 Cryptococcus
8 Candida albicans
9 Toxoplasma gondii

Questions
Which of the agents above lead to the following situations in patients with HIV/AIDS?

a. Kaposi's sarcoma.

b. Intracerebral lymphoma.

c. Odynophagia

d. Treatment with rifampicin, isoniazid, pyrazinamide and ethambutol is required.

e. The most common type of pneumonia.

f. Retinitis.

g. India ink stain on cerebrospinal fluid (CSF) is diagnostic.

81 Gram negative infections   ID

Options
1 Enterobacter
2 Pertussis
3 Haemophilus influenzae
4 Pseudomonas aeruginosa
5 Mycoplasma
6 Chlamydial infection

Questions
Pick the best option:

a. Was a major cause of meningitis before a vaccination was introduced.

b. Most infections are caused by type b.

c. Salmonella is an example.

d. Symptoms include an increasingly severe and paroxysmal cough in spasms of coughing followed by a 'whoop'.

e. Symptoms include a dry persistent cough with or without joint pains. A chest x ray shows bilateral, patchy consolidation.

82 Vaccinations ID

Options
1 Pertussis
2 Diptheria
3 Tetanus
4 Haemophilus influenza B
5 Polio
6 Measles/mumps/rubella (MMR)
7 Bacillus Calmette-Guérin (BCG)
8 Influenza
9 Pneumovax®
10 Hepatitis B

Questions
Pick the best answer

a. All people over 65 years require this vaccination annually.

b. Should only be given if tuberculin test is negative

c. There was some controversy surrounding autism and Crohn's disease.

d. Oral vaccination in the UK has been stopped.

e. Should be avoided in those who are immunosuppressed.

f. Contraindicated in those with anaphylactic reaction to eggs.

83 Vaccines   ID

Options

1   Pneumococcal
2   Hepatits A
3   Hepatitis B
4   Meningococcal
5   Chicken pox and herpes zoster immunisation
6   Rabies
7   MMR
8   Typhoid
9   Yellow fever
10 Japanese B encephalitis

Questions

Pick the best option

a. This should be offered to sex workers.

b. This vaccination prevents a mosquito-borne viral infection.
    It is unlicensed in the UK.

c. Vaccination available for type A and C disease but not type B.

d. Recommended for those without a spleen.

e. Should not be given to those allergic to neomycin, kanamycin and
    polymyxin.

84 Congenital infections in childhood ID

Options
1 CMV infection
2 Herpes simplex infection
3 Parvovirus
4 Rubella
5 Syphillis
6 Toxoplasmosis

Questions
Pick the most likely congenital infection responsible:

a. A newborn child with thrombocytopenia, hepatosplenomegaly, retinitis and periventricular calcification on CT scan of the head.

b. A newborn girl with hepatosplenomegaly, chorioretinitis and tram-like calcifications on CT scan of the head.

c. A stillborn child with non-immune hydrops fetalis.

d. An infant with skeletal changes suggestive of recurrent periostitis, a bony prominence of the head and a saddle nose.

85 | Vaccines | ID

Options
1 Haemophilus influenzae B
2 Mantoux
3 Pneumovax
4 Rubella
5 Salk Polio
6 Tetanus

Questions
Which vaccine is of the following type?

a. Killed.

b. Conjugate.

c. Live.

d. Polysaccharide.

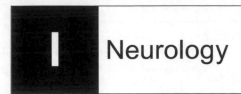

I Neurology

86 Lesions in the nervous system   NEURO

Options
1 Spinal cord
2 Frontal lobe
3 Parietal lobe
4 Occipital lobe
5 Temporal lobe
6 Cerebellum
7 Medulla
8 Pons

Questions
Match the following clinical features with the most likely site of pathology.

a. Disinhibition.

b. Cortical deafness.

c. Impaired musical perception.

d. Homonymous superior quadrantanopia.

e. Cortical blindness.

f. Apraxia.

g. Acalculia.

h. Astereognosis.

87 Cranial nerve   NEURO

Options
1. II
2. III
3. IV
4. V
5. VI
6. VII
7. VIII
8. IX and X
9. XI
10. XII

Questions
For each of the following, which cranial nerve applies?

a. A lesion leads to ptosis, mydriasis and an eye positioned downwards and laterally.

b. The tongue will deviate to the side of any lesion.

c. It is needed for the gag reflex.

d. A lesion will lead to diplopia on lateral gaze.

e. A posterior communicating artery aneurysm can lead to a palsy of this nerve.

f. Bell's palsy is a lower motor neurone lesion of this nerve.

g. Frusemide may affect this nerve.

h. The patient is unable to shrug shoulders against resistance when this nerve is damaged.

88 Mononeuropathy   NEURO

Options
1 Median nerve
2 Ulnar nerve
3 Radial nerve
4 Sciatic nerve
5 Common peroneal nerve
6 Tibial nerve

Questions
Which nerve is involved?

a. This nerve opens the fist.

b. Provides sensation over the sole.

c. A lesion may cause foot drop and loss of sensation over the dorsum of the foot.

d. Provides sensation over the dorsal aspect of the root of the thumb.

e. Involved in carpal tunnel syndrome.

f. Needed to abduct the fingers.

g. Needed to stand on tiptoe.

89 Headache   NEURO

Options
1. Meningitis
2. Encephalitis
3. Subarachnoid haemorrhage
4. Head injury
5. Sinusitis
6. Dental caries
7. Migraine
8. Cluster headache
9. Trigeminal neuralgia
10. Temporal arteritis

Questions
Which of the above conditions are most likely to give the following features?

a. A very sudden onset headache with a stiff neck.

b. Aura, visual disturbance, nausea and vomiting associated with the headache, usually only on one side of the head.

c. Intense stabbing pain lasting seconds in just one region on the face.

d. Scalp tenderness with a raised erythrocyte sedimentation rate (ESR).

e. Fever, photophobia, with neck stiffness and rash.

f. Fever, confusion and decreased conscious level are associated with this headache. An electro encephalogram (EEG) may aid diagnosis.

Obstetrics & Gynaecology

90 Cervical cytology O&G

Options
1 Repeat in 3 years
2 Repeat in 6 years
3 Repeat in 6 months
4 Repeat in 4 months
5 Colposcopy
6 Urgent colposcopy
7 Reassure
8 Repeat in 2 years
9 Repeat in 1 year
10 Repeat in 9 months

Questions
Concerning screening for cervical cancer, what is the most appropriate action?

a. A normal smear result.

b. Inflammatory smear result.

c. Abnormal glandular cells.

d. Moderate dyskaryosis.

e. Severe dyskaryosis.

91 Male infertility   O&G

Options
 1 16-17 %
 2 4 %
 3 87%
 4 2%
 5 53%
 6 Less than 1%
 7 72%

Questions
What percentage of male infertility is caused by the following?

a. Gonadotrophin deficiency.

b. Genital tract obstruction.

c. Congenital.

d. Genital tract infection.

e. Varicocele.

f. Asthenozoospermia.

g. Teratozoospermia.

92 Gynaecological surgery   O&G

Options
1. Hysterectomy
2. Manchester repair
3. Dilatation and curettage
4. Hysteroscopy
5. Hysteroscopic endometrial ablation
6. Laparoscopy
7. Colporrhaphy

Questions
Which surgical procedure is referred in each of the following statements?

a. Used to treat laxity of the vaginal wall.

b. This artificially induces an Asherman's syndrome.

c. The cervix is amputated and the uterus is supported by shortening the ligaments.

d. The commonest outpatient and inpatient procedure on the list.

e. It is named the Wertheim's type if extended to local lymph nodes and a cuff of the vagina.

93 Minor symptoms of pregnancy.   O&G

Options
1 Headaches
2 Fainting
3 Abdominal pain
4 Carpal tunnel syndrome
5 Heartburn
6 Backache
7 Itch
8 Ankle swelling
9 Leg cramps
10 Chloasma

Questions
Pick the best choice from the list

a. Due to hormones causing weakening of ligaments and extra strain.

b. If affecting the soles of the feet and palms of the hands, liver function tests should be carried out.

c. Rest and leg-elevation helps but pre-eclampsia needs to be excluded.

d. Causes a tingling sensation in the fingers.

e. This is a patch of increased skin pigmentation.

f. Occurs partly because of pyloric sphincter relaxation.

94 Nausea and vomitting in early pregnancy   **O&G**

Options
1 Beneficial
2 Likely to be beneficial
3 Unknown effectiveness
4 Likely to be ineffective or harmful
5 Trade off between benefit and harm

Questions
According to clinical evidence, BMJ, what best describes these treatments?

a. Ginger.

b. Acupuncture.

c. Phenothiazines.

d. Acupressure.

e. H1 antagonists.

f. Vitamin B12.

g. Vitamin B6

95 Birth injuries to the neonate   O&G

Options
1. Moulding
2. Cephalhaematoma
3. Erb's palsy
4. Subaponeurotic haematoma
5. Skull fractures
6. Intracranial injuries
7. Caput succadaneum
8. Klumpke's palsy

Questions
Pick the most likely injury

a. Blood lies between the aponeurosis and the periosteum.

b. The hand is in a 'porter's tip' posture.

c. Oedematous swelling of the scalp, superficial to the cranial periosteum.

d. Natural process where the bones override each other.

e. Subperiostial swelling on the foetal head.

96 Prenatal diagnosis   O&G

Options
1 Ultrasound
2 Alpha-fetoprotein (AFP)
3 Amniocentesis
4 Chorionic villus sampling
5 Fetoscopy
6 Triple test

Questions
For each of the following statements, pick the most likely test from the list above.

a. Best at picking up structural problems.

b. Usually occurs at 16 weeks, samples can be taken and sent for karyotyping and enzyme or gene probe analysis.

c. Can occur after 10 weeks and the placenta is sampled.

d. A glycoprotein synthesised by the foetal liver and gastro-intestinal tract.

e. This blood test involves maternal AFP, unconjugated oestriol and total human chorionic gonadotrophin.

97 Contraception - Pearl index   O&G

Options
1. 0 - 0.05
2. 0 - 0.5
3. 0.1
4. 0.2 - 3.0
5. 0.3 - 4
6. 4 - 20
7. 5 - 15

Questions
What is the failure rate of these methods of contraception per 100 woman-years?

a. Male sterilisation.

b. Diaphragm.

c. Female condom.

d. Injectables.

e. Progesterone only pill.

f. Combined oral contraceptive pill.

98 Contraception methods   O&G

Options
1 Persona ®
2 Femidom
3 Combined oral contraceptive pill
4 Progesterone only pill
5 Cerazette ®
6 Implanon ®
7 Mirena ®
8 Depot progestogen
9 Intrauterine device
10 Diaphragm

Questions
Pick the most relevant form of contraception.

a. Migraine with aura is an absolute contraindication.

b. Not suitable for chaotic lifestyle since it requires the strictest attention to time-keeping.

c. Its main effect is on the endometrium.

d. Not suitable for women with very irregular periods.

e. Is licensed for use as emergency contraception up to five days after unprotected intercourse within 19 days of a 28-day period.

f. Has the greatest protection against STIs.

g. Can be termed a "natural" method of contraception.

h. Its action is mainly to cause an ovulation.

99   Medical problems in pregnancy   O&G

Options
1 Eclampsia
2 Diabetes
3 Hypothyroidism
4 Epilepsy
5 Cardiac disease
6 Asthma
7 Prolactinomas
8 Hyperthyroidism

Questions
Choose the most likely medical problem.

a. Bromocriptine is used to treat this condition.

b. Patients with Marfan's syndrome may have this medical problem.

c. Folic acid is very important in these patients.

d. There is an increased incidence of haemorrhagic disease of the newborn.

e. The most common form is Hashimoto's.

100 Sexually transmitted infections   O&G

Options
1 Neisseria gonorrhoea
2 Chlamydia trachomatis
3 Treponema pallidum
4 Bacterial vaginosis
5 Herpes simplex virus
6 Human papilloma virus
7 Hepatitis B
8 Hepatitis C
9 HIV
10 Trichomonas vaginalis

Questions
Pick the best answer.

a. This is a parasitic infection.

b. This causes warts.

c. This is the commonest cause of vaginal discharge.

d. Gardnerella vaginalis is associated with this.

e. This is the most common sexually transmitted infection in the UK.

101 Gynaecological Infections   O&G

Options
1 Molluscum contagiosum
2 Trichomonas vaginalis
3 Pediculosis pubis
4 Scabies
5 Bacterial vaginosis
6 Candida

Questions
Pick the best answer.

a. Classically causes a grey discharge with a fishy odour.

b. This can cause a hypertrophic/papular rash on genital skin.

c. Treated with vaginal imidazoles or oral fluconazole.

d. Caused by a large pox virus.

e. This can lead to a frothy fishy discharge, severe vulvovaginitis and 'strawberry' cervicitis.

f. Causes burrow track marks in the skin.

g. Treated with malathion.

102 Menorrhagia treatment   O&G

Options
1 Mirena® intra-uterine system
2 Danazol
3 Tranexamic acid
4 Mefenamic acid
5 Ethamsylate
6 Progesterones

Questions
Which treatment of menorrhagia is best described by each of the following statements?

a. Therapy is stopped after 5 years.

b. Given usually as 1 gram tds during menstruation.

c. Interacts with anti-coagulants, anti-epileptics and cyclosporins.

d. Usually given as 200 mg once a day for 3 months.

e. Anatomical variance of the uterine cavity may be a contra-indication to this treatment.

103 Uterine problems   O&G

Options
1 Fibroids
2 Endometrial proliferation
3 Endometrial carcinoma
4 Endometritis
5 Cervicitis
6 Retained products of conception

Questions
Pick the best option.

a. Anovulatory cycles is a cause.

b. Surgery or childbirth are the most common contributory factors.

c. Often treated with both doxycycline and metronidazole.

d. Must be excluded if there is post menopausal bleeding.

e. Benign tumour of the smooth muscle.

104 Symptoms   O&G

Options
1 Primary amenorrhoea
2 Secondary amenorrhoea
3 Menorrhagia
4 Dysmenorrhoea
5 Oligomenorrhoea
6 Dyspareunia
7 Postcoital bleeding
8 Post menopausal bleeding
9 Menarche

Questions
What term best describes these sentences?

a. Failure to start having periods.

b. Excessive blood loss.

c. Painful periods.

d. The periods stop for a period greater than six months and the woman is not pregnant.

e. Bleeding after sexual intercourse.

105 Lower genital tract problems   O&G

Options
1 Pruritus vulvae
2 Lichen sclerosis
3 Leukoplakia
4 Carcinoma of vulva
5 Folliculitis
6 Urethral caruncle
7 Bartholin's cyst
8 Vulval herpes simplex
9 Lichen planus

Questions
Pick the best clinical situation

a. This may be caused by infections or chemicals.

b. Human Papilloma virus is the main causative agent.

c. Marsupialisation is a treatment option.

d. This is characterised by intensely itchy white patches around the vulva with loss of architecture and fusion of the clitoral head.

e. Painful ulceration is common.

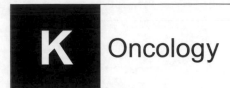

K Oncology

106 Ovarian tumours · ONCOL

Options
1. Polycystic ovarian syndrome
2. Serous cystadenomas
3. Mucinous cystadenomas
4. Fibromas
5. Teratomas
6. Other germ cell tumours
7. Sex-cord tumours
8. Functional cysts

Questions
Pick the most likely pathology.

a. Non-gestational choriocarcinomas are an example.

b. Arise from cortical mesenchyme.

c. Associated with Meig's syndrome, they are small, solid, benign fibrous tissue tumours.

d. These are the commonest large ovarian tumours filled with proteinaceous material.

e. These are very common and considered normal if less than 5 cm.

107 Cancers with associated clinical syndromes ONCOL

Options
1 Neurofibromatosis
2 Von Hippel-Lindau
3 Porphyria cutanea tarda
4 Polyposis coli
5 Gardener's syndrome
6 Peutz-Jegher's syndrome
7 Ataxia telangiectasia
8 Albinism
9 IgA deficiency
10 IgM deficiency

Questions
Match the disease to each of the following tumour susceptibilities:

a. Glioma.

b. Carcinoma of the stomach.

c. Renal cell carcinoma.

d. Hepatocellular carcinoma.

e. Basal cell carcinoma.

f. Squamous cell carcinoma.

g. Phaeochromocytoma.

108 Epidermal tumours   **ONCOL**

Options
1 Papilloma
2 Seborrhoeic keratosis
3 Solar keratosis
4 Bowen's disease
5 Marjolin's ulcer
6 Basal cell carcinoma
7 Squamous cell carcinoma

Questions
Choose the most likely epidermal tumour.

a. Microscopically solid sheets of uniform darkly staining cells arising from the basal layer of the skin are seen. Prickle cells and epithelial pearls are both absent.

b. Macroscopically the tumour has a raised, rolled edge. It consists of pearly nodules over which fine blood vessels can be seen.

c. It is the most common form of skin cancer in white people.

d. This is small, hard, brown scaly tumour on sun exposed areas of skin of the elderly.

e. This is a common, benign, pedunculated tumour often pigmented with melanin.

109 Intracranial tumours   ONCOL

Options
1 Astrocytomas
2 Cerebral lymphoma
3 Meningioma
4 Acoustic neuroma
5 Pituitary tumour
6 Craniopharyngioma
7 Secondary tumour
8 Medulloblastomas
9 Ependymomas
10 Oligodendrogliomas

Questions
Choose the most likely answer.

a. These arise from the lining cells of the ventricles, the central canal of the spinal cord or the choroid plexus.

b. This the most common type of glioma.

c. These are rapidly growing small-cell tumours generally affecting the cerebellum in children.

d. These arise from the arachnoid cells in the dura matter.

e. Chromophobe, eosinophil and basophil adenomas are subtypes.

f. Tinnitus and hearing loss are classical presenting symptoms.

g. The most common intracranial tumour.

110 Common malignancies death rate ONCOL

Options
1 1,000
2 5,000
3 10,000
4 15,000
5 20,000
6 35,000
7 50,000
8 100,000

Questions
What is the closest approximation to the number of deaths per annum in the UK for the following cancers?

a. Stomach.

b. Lymphoma.

c. Pancreas.

d. Lung.

e. Prostate.

f. Breast.

g. Colorectal.

111 Tumour markers   ONCOL

Options
1 Prostate specific antigen
2 CA-125
3 Alpha feto protein
4 Carcinoembryonic antigen
5 Paraproteins

Questions
Which of the options above are used as marker for these diseases?

a. Myelomatosis.

b. Colorectal cancer.

c. Testicular teratoma.

d. Prostatic carcinoma.

e. Hepatoma.

112 Cancers of the tropics ONCOL

Options
1 Oropharyngeal cancer
2 Nasopharyngeal cancer
3 Primary upper small intestinal lymphoma
4 Burkitt's lymphoma
5 Kaposi's sarcoma
6 Oesophageal carcinoma

Questions
Pick the best match

a. This is associated with HIV infection. It has cutaneous and viceral manifestations.

b. Core needle biopsy confirms the diagnosis with 'starry sky' appearance on histology.

c. A tumour of children associated with mosquito-borne Epstein-Barr virus.

d. Associated with cell-mediated immune deficiency from malnutrition and chronic diarrhoeal disease.

e. Associated with cultural habit of chewing and retaining betel quid in the mouth. (Note: The habit of chewing betel quid is widespread in South-East Asia and the South Pacific islands and in people of Indian origin elsewhere in the world. Betel quid usually contains areca nut, lime and catechu wrapped in a betel leaf. Tobacco is often added)

113 Childhood cancer ONCOL

Options
1 Retinoblastoma
2 Brain tumour
3 Neuroblastoma
4 Bone tumours
5 Leukaemia
6 Lymphoma
7 Wilm's tumour
8 Rhabdomyosarcoma
9 Germ cell tumour

Questions
Pick the most likely cancer involved.

a. This usually presents with a renal mass.

b. Arises from mesenchymal tissue.

c. Examples are sacrococcygeal and gonadal tumours.

d. Arises from neural crest tissue.

e. Is suspected if the red reflex is absent.

L Ophthalmology

114 Eye muscles   OPHTH

Options
1 Medial rectus
2 Lateral rectus
3 Superior rectus
4 Inferior rectus
5 Superior oblique
6 Inferior oblique
7 Levator palpebrae superioris
8 Muller's muscle

Questions
Which is the correct eye muscle?

a. Is innervated by the trochlear nerve.

b. Elevates the upper lid and is innervated by the cervical sympathetics.

c. If not intact, will cause a marked ptosis.

d. Is innervated by the 6th cranial nerve.

e. Moves the eye nasally.

f. Moves the eye temporally.

115 | Occular findings in systemic disease | OPHTH

Options
1 AIDS/HIV
2 Albinism
3 Alkaptonuria
4 Amyloidosis
5 Anaemia
6 Ankylosing spondylitis
7 Alport's syndrome
8 Behçet 's syndrome
9 Crohn's disease
10 Cystic fibrosis

Questions
Match the most likely disease.

a. The background to the fundus is pale.

b. This results in melanin deposits in the sclera.

c. CMV retinitis is associated with this.

d. This disease will cause weakness of extraocular muscles, vitreous opacities, and nodules in the lids and conjunctiva.

e. This can lead to cataracts and keratoconus.

116 Systemic disease   OPHTH

Options
1 Diabetes mellitus
2 Cystinosis
3 Dermatomyositis
4 Down's syndrome
5 Ehlers-Danlos syndrome
6 Friedrich's ataxia
7 Gout
8 Herpes zoster
9 Homocystinuria
10 Hyperparathyroidism

Questions
Match the most likely disease.

a. Band keratopathy (grey-white band, containing calcium deposits, extending horizontally across the cornea) and optic atrophy.

b. The lens is dislocated inferiorly.

c. Dermatitis along ophthalmic branch of cranial nerve 5, keratitis and uveitis.

d. Blue sclera, strabismus and epicanthal folds.

e. Signs include Brushfield's spots, myopia, strabismus.

117 Systemic disease

Options
1 Kernicterus
2 Migraine
3 Multiple sclerosis
4 Neurofibromatosis
5 Osteogenesis imperfecta
6 Pseudoxanthoma elasticum
7 Reiters syndrome
8 Riley-Day syndrome
9 Rubella
10 Sarcoid

Questions
Match the most likely disease.

a. Angioid streaks

b. Lid and orbital tumours and optic glioma.

c. Retrobulbar neuritis, optic atrophy, internuclear ophthalmoplegia.

d. Throbbing eye pain, transient visual compromise.

e. Decreased tear production, decreased corneal sensation with
    subsequent exposure keratitis.

118 Systemic disease   OPHTH

Options
1 Stevens-Johnson syndrome
2 Bacterial endocarditis
3 Sturge-Weber disease
4 Treponema pallidum infection
5 Wilson's disease
6 Giant cell arteritis
7 Toxoplasmosis
8 Tuberous sclerosis
9 Vitamin A deficiency
10 Wilm's tumour

Questions
Match the most likely disease.

a. Aniridia.

b. Night blindness.

c. Retinal tumours.

d. Chorioretinitis.

e. Congenital glaucoma on side of facial naevus.

f. Argyll-Robertson pupil.

g. Roth spots.

119 Drug effects OPHTH

Options

1 Amiodarone
2 Digoxin
3 Ethambutol
4 Chloroquine
5 Haloperidol
6 Steroids
7 Tamoxifen
8 Viagra
9 Vitamin D intoxication
10 Vitamin A intoxication

Questions

Identify the drug that most causes these eye problems.

a. Refractile crystals in the cornea.

b. 'Blue-tinged' vision.

c. Band keratopathy.

d. Corneal pigment whorl.

e. Yellow vision.

f. Retrobulbar neuritis with decreased colour vision and visual acuity.

120 Eye signs   **OPHTH**

Options
1 Stye
2 Chalazion
3 Blepharitis
4 Xanthelasmata
5 Ectropion
6 Subconjunctival haemorrhage
7 Dacryoadenitis
8 Pinguecula
9 Corneal abrasion
10 Acute glaucoma

Questions
Match the most likely disease to the eye signs described.

a. Spontaneously appearing patch of redness over sclera. It is painless and vision is normal.

b. Slightly tender smooth well defined lump, a distance away from the lid margin.

c. Warm, painful swelling, acutely arising, in superolateral aspect of upper lid.

d. Entire eye is very painful, hazy vision, halos around lights, mid-dilated pupil.

e. Soft, yellowish superficial skin lesions in a patient with hyperlipidaemia.

f. Crusty, mildly sore eyelids, eyelids stick together in the morning.

121 Retina problems   OPHTH

Options
1 Old inactive choroidoretinitis
2 Retinoblastoma
3 Roth spots
4 Papilloedema
5 Retinitis pigmentosa
6 Retinal detachment
7 Senile macular degeneration
8 Cholesterol emboli
9 Benign pigment crescent
10 Diabetic retinopathy

Questions
Match each of the following descriptions with the most likely retinal problem.

a. Microaneurysms, dot haemorrrhages, blot haemorrhages, cotton wool spots and hard exudates.

b. Attacks of amaurosis fugax in the left eye and intermittent episodes of weakness on the right side of the body. Glistening deposits are seen at areas of arteriolar bifurcation.

c. Progressive loss of visual acuity in an elderly patient with pigment, exudates and haemorrhages in the the foveal region.

d. Progressive difficulty in seeing at night followed by tunnel vision. Black pigment with the appearance of 'bone-spicule' is seen in the peripheral retina.

122 Ptosis	OPHTH

Options
1 Neurogenic
2 Myogenic
3 Aponeurotic
4 Mechanical
5 Congenital

Questions
For each of the following conditions, select the most likely cause of ptosis from the list above.

a. Tumour of the upper eye lids.

b. Poorly developed levator palpebrae muscle.

c. Blepharochalasis.

d. Myasthenia gravis.

e. Horner's syndrome.

f. Tabes dorsalis

g. Marcus Gunn syndrome

123 Systemic eye disease OPHTH

Options
1 Rheumatoid arthritis
2 Giant cell arteritis
3 Psoriasis
4 Behçet's disease
5 Dermatomyositis
6 Wegener's granulomatosis
7 Polyarteritis nodosa
8 Sturge-Weber syndrome
9 Systemic lupus erythematosus
10 Neurofibromatosis

Questions
Select the disease with the following eye signs.

a. Optic nerve glioma and café au lait spots on the eyelids.

b. Unilateral port wine stain (haemangioma) over the eyelids and forehead.

c. Purple heliotrope rash on the eyelids.

d. Recurrent iritis, associated with HLA B5. Commonly associated with a Turkish or Mediterranean origin.

e. Treatment with psoralen derivatives and UVA may cause lid erythema or keratitis.

124 Ocular side effects of systemic drugs OPHTH

Options

1 Erythema multiforme
2 Lupus erythomatosus-like syndrome
3 Oculomucocutaneous syndrome
4 Verticillata
5 Corneal deposits
6 Transient myopia
7 Cataract
8 Failure of accommodation

Questions

Match the appropriate side effect to each of the following drugs.

a. Hydralazine.

b. Penicillin.

c. Practolol.

d. Chloroquine.

e. Steroids.

f. Tetracycline.

125 HLA associations.   **OPHTH**

Options
 1 HLA-A11
 2 HLA-A29
 3 HLA-B5
 4 HLA-B7
 5 HLA-B8
 6 HLA-DR2
 7 HLA-DR3
 8 HLA-DR4
 9 HLA-B27
10 HLA-BW5

Questions
Pick the HLA associations for these conditions that can affect the eyes.

a. Ankylosing spondylitis.

b. Systemic lupus erythematosus.

c. Myasthenia gravis.

d. Seropositive rheumatoid arthritis

e. Multiple sclerosis.

f. Behcet's disease.

126 Sudden loss of vision   OPHTH

Options
1 Toxoplasmosis
2 Temporal arteritis
3 Amaurosis fugax
4 Central serous retinopathy
5 Branch retinal vein occlusion
6 Central retinal artery occlusion
7 Retinal detachment
8 Glaucoma
9 Nuclear cataract
10 Central retinal vein occlusion

Questions
For each of these scenarios, which is the most likely diagnosis?

a. A patient presents with a sudden unilateral painless loss of vision which lasted just a few minutes and then completely resolved.

b. A 70 year-old patient complains of sudden, unilateral loss of vision with associated scalp tenderness, jaw claudication and proximal muscle pain.

c. On fundoscopy, there is a wedge-shaped area of microaneurysms, blot and flame haemorrhages, and cotton wool spots.

d. A patient reports flashing lights or spots in their field of vision followed by sudden, painless, unilateria loss of vision. "Floaters" may be experienced.

e. On fundoscopy there is a diffuse milky white retina with a "cherry-red" spot at the macular.

127 Visual field defects   OPHTH

Options
1 Morning glory syndrome
2 Anterior ischaemic optic neuropathy
3 Tilted optic discs
4 Retinitis pigmentosa
5 Acute (closed angle) glaucoma
6 Pituitary adenoma
7 Toxic optic neuropathy
8 Right temporal lobe lesion
9 Left parietal lobe lesion
10 Chronic simple (open angle) glaucoma

Questions
From these scenarios which is the most likely diagnosis?

a. A patient complains of progressive loss of visual acuity over hours or days. There is a unilateral altitudinal visual field defect, the optic nerve is swollen and there is reduced colour vision in the affected eye.

b. A patient has marked peripheral loss of their vision on visual field testing and there is severe cupping of the optic nerve.

c. A bitemporal visual field defect is found on visual field testing.

d. A left superior homonymous quadrantanopia is found on visual field testing.

e. A right inferior homonymous quadrantanopia is found on visual field testing.

128 Red eye   OPHTH

Options
1 Uveitis
2 Episcleritis
3 Hordeolum
4 Acanthamoeba keratitis
5 Entropion
6 Orbital cellulitis
7 Herpes simplex keratitis
8 Blepharitis
9 Scleritis
10 Allergic conjunctivitis

Questions
From these scenarios which is the most likely diagnosis?

a. A patient with seropositive rheumatoid arthritis complains of intense eye pain and redness. Slit lamp examination reveals a purple injection which does not blanch with 2.5% topical phenylephrine.

b. A patient is noted to have periorbital swelling and erythema, with fever and painful eye movements.

c. A patient has recurrent episodes of sudden unilateral red eye with mild discomfort. Slit lamp examination reveals a discrete area of conjunctival injection and the superficial episcleral vessels blanch with 2.5% phenylephrine.

d. A contact lens wearer with a history of rinsing their lenses with water complains of severe pain, photophobia and reduced vision. Slit lamp examination shows lid oedema, conjunctival injection and a ring of infiltrates in the stroma.

e. A person has red, itchy eyes which are relieved by topical antihistamines.

129 Mydriasis   OPHTH

Options
1 Horner's syndrome
2 Latent nystagmus
3 Pharmocologic mydriasis
4 Holmes-Adie pupil
5 Third nerve palsy
6 Sixth nerve palsy
7 Acute (closed angle) glaucoma
8 Fourth nerve palsy
9 Iritis
10 Trauma related pupil dilation

Questions
From these scenarios which is the most likely diagnosis?

a. A patient presents with diplopia and unilateral ptosis. The eye on the affected side looks down and out. The pupil is fixed and dilated.

b. A patient complains of dull eye pain, blurred vision and sees halos around lights. They are nauseated and have a fixed, mid-dilated pupil, with a hazy cornea and a red eye.

c. A patient has signs of iris atrophy and sphincter rupture in their fixed dilated pupil.

d. A patient has recently been handling belladonna plants in their garden. They now notice that one of their pupils is dilated and experience photophobia and blurring of near vision.

e. A young female patient has a unilateral dilated pupil which responds slowly to light and accommodation

130 Anisocoria   OPHTH

Options
1 Physiological anisocoria
2 Iritis
3 Duane's syndrome
4 Graves' disease
5 Coats' disease
6 Argyll-Robertson pupil
7 Pharmocologic miosis
8 Congenital hypertrophy of the retinal pigment epithelium
9 Horner's syndrome
10 Holmes-Adie pupil

Questions
From these scenarios which is the most likely diagnosis?

a. A patient is noted to have unilateral partial ptosis, unilateral miosis with no dilation of the affected pupil in dim light and an ipsilateral loss of facial sweating.

b. A patient is currently being treated for glaucoma and complains of unilateral blurred vision and a dull ache on the affected side.

c. A patient presents with acute eye pain, photophobia, blurred vision and lacrimation with a red eye. A hypopyon may be seen.

d. A patient has been aware of a difference of 0.5mm in size between their two pupils from a young age. Both pupils respond normally to light and near testing. The anisocoria is equal under photopic and scotopic conditions.

e. Eye examination reveals pupils that are irregular, react poorly to light but accomodate normally.

131 Cornea and conjunctiva   OPHTH

Options
1 Acanthamoeba keratitis
2 Lyme disease
3 Corneal arcus
4 Pinguecula
5 Vernal conjunctivitis
6 Recurrent corneal erosion
7 Herpes simplex keratitis
8 Pterygium
9 Keratoconus
10 Fungal keratitis

Questions
From these scenarios which is the most likely diagnosis?

a. A 75 year old has noticed a 'white ring around the coloured part of their eye.' On examination, opacification of the peripheral cornea is seen.

b. On ocular examination you see a triangular band of fibrovascular tissue growth with the apex on the cornea and the broad band on the temporal bulbar conjunctiva.

c. With slit-lamp examination, a ring of brown pigment around the base of a conical shaped cornea is seen. There is also a deviation of the lower lid during downward gaze caused by the protruding apex of the cone (Munson's sign).

d. An asymptomatic patient has yellow-white, slightly elevated lesions nasally and temporally on the bulbar conjunctiva but there is no direct involvement of the cornea.

e. A patient who is prone to getting coldsores complains of pain, irritation, photophobia and excessive tearing. Fluorescein staining reveals dendritic lesions on the cornea.

132 Anomalies of globe position OPHTH

Options
1 Cavernous hemangioma
2 Thyroid eye disease
3 Cavernous sinus arteriovenous malformation
4 Xanthelasma
5 Phthisis bulbi
6 Kaposi's sarcoma
7 Orbital blow out fracture
8 Orbital cellulitis
9 Axial myopia
10 Rhabdomyosarcoma

Questions
From these scenarios which is the most likely diagnosis?

a. A 30 year old woman has symptoms of diplopia and is noted to have unilateral proptosis with lid lag. Refraction reveals a hyperopic shift.

b. A patient has recently been hit by a ball and complains of diplopia, pain on eye movement and local tenderness. The eye is enophthalmic.

c. A patient is suffering from dry eyes and frequent blinking. They have retracted lids with lid lag on downgaze, bilateral proptosis and restriction of the extraocular muscles in upgaze.

d. A patient complains of fever, pain, swollen reddish eyelids, diplopia, eye redness, blurred vision, pain on eye movement and proptosis.

e. A male has recently had a severe head trauma. His conjunctiva is brick red and extrudes over the lower lid. The affected eye is pulsatile.

133 Systemic conditions associated with ocular signs   OPHTH

Options
1 Tuberculosis
2 Marfan's syndrome
3 Sarcoidosis
4 Sickle cell disease
5 Diabetes mellitus
6 Myasthenia Gravis
7 Albinism
8 Hypertension
9 Multiple sclerosis
10 Weill-Marchesani syndrome

Questions
From these scenarios which is the most likely diagnosis?

a. A patient with no ocular symptoms is fatigued, dehydrated and suffers frequent infections. On fundus examination salmon-patch intra-retinal haemorrhages, black sunbursts, venous tortusity and angiod streaks are seen.

b. Fundoscopy shows flame haemorrhages, exudates forming a macula star, arterial constriction and macro-aneurysms.

c. Fundoscopy shows blot haemorrhages, microaneuryms, cotton-wool spots, venous beading and intraretinal microvascular abnormalities.

d. A patient with pale, depigmented skin and hair complains of blurred vision, photophobia and skin photosensitivity

e. A tall adolescent patient with a high arched palate is noted to be highly myopic with upward lens dislocation.

134 Eye pain and drugs   OPHTH

Options
1 Aciclovir 800mg 5 times a day
2 Prednisolone 0.5% drops every 2 hours
3 Leave for 4 days before re-assessment
4 Cyclopentolate 0.5% 1-2 drops 6-hourly
5 Pilocarpine 2-4% drops hourly
6 Cetazolamide 500mg orally stat

Questions
Which is the most suitable treatment option from the list above for each of the following scenarios?

a. A patient enters your clinic complaining of pain, tingling and numbness around the eye with a unilateral blistering inflammatory rash in a well demarcated area over the eyelid and forehead.

b. A patient complains of sudden acute photophobia, blurred vision and has a positive Talbot's test. Other than resorting to steroids, what other treatment would you consider?

c. A patient complains of pain, nausea and vomiting and presents with a fixed dilated pupil. The eyeball feels hard on palpation. From your diagnostic suspicions what would be your first line treatment for this patient?

d. These are potentially dangerous drugs to use in the eyes as they may cause progression of dendritic ulcers.

135 Eye signs in medical disorders OPHTH

Options
1 Lisch nodules
2 Brushfield spots
3 Kayser-Fleischer rings
4 Bitot's spots
5 Corneal arcus
6 Blue sclera
7 Corneal calcification

Questions
Which eyes signs do these disorders cause?

a. Osteogenesis imperfecta

b. Sarcoidosis

c. Neurofibromatosis

d. Down's syndrome

e. Vitamin A deficiency

f. Old Age

g. Marfan's syndrome

136 Hypertensive retinopathy   OPHTH

Options
1 Grade 1
2 Grade 2
3 Grade 3
4 Grade 4

Questions
Which grade do these changes in hypertensive retinopathy belong to?

a. Papilloedema

b. Focal arteriolar attenuation

c. Arteriovenous nipping

d. Silver wiring

e. Haemorrhages

f. Hard exudates

g. Cotton wool spots

137 Eye conditions. **OPHTH**

Options
1 Papilloedema
2 Optic atrophy
3 Neuritis
4 Choroidoretinitis
5 Cataracts
6 Iritis
7 Ptosis
8 Uveitis

Questions
Choose the most likely eye problem.

a. Third nerve palsy causes this.

b. Associated with ankylosing spondylitis.

c. Associated with sarcoidosis.

d. Ethambutol causes this.

e. Toxoplasmosis causes this.

f. Central vein thrombosis will cause this.

g. Space occupying lesion is an important cause.

h. Carbon dioxide retention may cause this

Orthopaedics

138 Fractures ORTHO

Options
1. Pouteau's fracture
2. Pott's fracture
3. Straddle fracture
4. Runner's fracture
5. Jefferson fracture
6. Shepherd's fracture
7. Smith's fracture
8. Rolando's fracture
9. Hangman's fracture
10. March fracture

Questions
Which fracture is being described in each of the statements below?

a. A blow to the top of the head may cause an unstable 'blowout' fracture of C1 (the ring of atlas).

b. May be seen in motor accidents where there is sudden forced hyperextension of the neck and subsequent fracture of the pedicle of C2.

c. A stress fracture of the metatarsal shaft after heavy and unaccustomed exercise.

d. This term applies to any ankle fracture, which may be subdivided into 'uni', 'bi' or 'trimalleolar'.

e. Another name for a Colles' fracture.

139 Musculoskeletal features of rheumatoid arthritis   ORTHO

Options
1 Symmetrical swelling of the metacarpophalangeal and proximal interphalangeal joints
2 'Swan neck' deformity
3 Boutonnière deformity
4 Z deformity of the thumb
5 Dorsal subluxation of the ulnar styloid of the wrist
6 Trigger finger
7 Carpal tunnel syndrome
8 Popliteal ('Baker's') cysts
9 Heberden's nodes

Questions
Pick the best option.

a. Which of the above does not feature in rheumatoid arthritis?

b. Which of the above may contribute to rupture of the 4th and 5th extensor tendons of the hand?

c. Anticoagulation of this complication may lead to compartment syndrome.

d. This complication may be due to nodules on the flexor tendon sheaths.

e. A patient complains of pain, tingling and numbness in the hand, especially at night and has noticed increasing clumsiness when picking up small objects.

140 Knee problems   ORTHO

Options
1 Iliotibial tract syndrome
2 Collateral ligament injury
3 Cruciate ligament injury
4 Meniscal tear
5 Meniscal cyst
6 Osteochondritis dissecans
7 Loose bodies in the knee
8 Osgood-Schlatter disease
9 Recurrent dislocation of the patella

Questions
Pick the best option.

a. Necrosis of articular cartilage and underlying bone.

b. A twisting injury of the knee is followed by immediate swelling and may be associated with 'locking' of the knee in partial flexion.

c. Suspect this if there is more than five degrees of lateral movement while stressing the knee into valgus or varus.

d. One mechanism of injury is a blow to the back of the tibia with or without rotation when the foot is fixed on the ground.

e. McMurray's and Apley's grinding test may detect this.

141 | Foot problems   ORTHO

Options
1 Pes planus
2 Pes cavus
3 Hammer toes
4 Claw toes
5 Hallux valgus
6 Hallux rigidus
7 Talipes equinovarus

Questions
Pick the best option.

a. Extended MTP joint, hyperflexed PIP joint and extended DIP joint.

b. Low medial arch.

c. Lateral deviation of the big toe at the MTP joint.

d. Extended MTP joint, flexion at PIP and DIP joints.

e. A large medial fat pad may create the appearance of this condition when a child first learns to walk.

f. May be associated with a chronic or congenital neurological condition.

Notes:
MTP = metatarsalphalangeal
PIP = proximal interphalangeal
DIP = distal interphalangeal

142 The painful foot   ORTHO

Options
1 Plantar fasciitis
2 Sever's disease
3 Frieberg's disease
4 Morton's metatarsalgia
5 Köhler's disease
6 Stress fracture

Questions
Pick the best option

a. Sharp pain in the forefoot, radiating to the toes, due to entrapment of the interdigital nerve between the metatarsals.

b. Osteochondritis of the navicular bone in children, leading to pain and tenderness over the dorsum of the midfoot.

c. The most common pain under the heel in a young adult. It is due to inflammation of the ligamentous tissue inserting into the calcaneum.

d. Softening and deformity of bone in children and adolescents that can lead to foot pain.

e. This form of osteochondritis is the most common cause of heel pain in children.

f. May be associated with Reiter's disease.

143 Compound fractures   ORTHO

Options
1 Type I
2 Type II
3 Type IIIA
4 Type IIIB
5 Type IIIC

Questions
Which type of compound fracture best fits each of the following descriptions?

a. A fracture with extensive soft tissue loss, periosteal stripping and exposure of bone.

b. A fracture where the wound is greater than 1cm, but is not associated with extensive soft tissue damage, tissue loss, or flap lacerations.

c. A fracture associated with vascular injury needing repair.

d. Either a fracture with adequate soft tissue coverage of bone, despite extensive soft tissue damage, or flap laceration, or any fracture involving high energy trauma or bone shattering regardless of wound size.

e. A fracture with a small, clean wound, less than 1cm long and little surrounding soft tissue damage.

144 Wrist fractures   ORTHO

Options
1 Colles' fracture
2 Smith's fracture
3 Barton's fracture
4 Isolated radial styloid fracture

Questions
Which type of fractures do the following descriptions relate to?

a. An unstable fracture-dislocation of the distal radius, where the distal fragment is tilted and displaced anteriorly and the fracture extends into the intra-articular joint.

b. A transverse fracture of the distal radius with dorsal displacement of the distal fragment.

c. Usually results from a fall onto an outstretched hand.

d. Usually follows a fall onto a flexed wrist.

e. May be caused by forced radial deviation of the wrist, for example during a fall.

145 Intracapsular fracture of the neck of femur ORTHO

Options
1 Garden I
2 Garden II
3 Garden III
4 Garden IV

Questions
Which radiological classification do each of these statements refer to?

a. Incomplete or impacted fracture of the femoral neck. The femoral trabeculae may be misaligned but the inferior cortex is intact.

b. Gross, often complete, displacement of the femoral head.

c. A complete fracture of the femoral neck with no displacement or misalignment of the trabeculao.

d. Obvious complete fracture line with slight displacement and/or rotation of the femoral head.

N Paediatrics

146 Interpretation of arterial blood gases   PAED

Options
1. Normal
2. Metabolic acidosis
3. Respiratory acidosis
4. Metabolic alkalosis
5. Respiratory alkalosis
6. None of the above

Questions
For each of the following scenarios, pick the most likely arterial blood gas result or correct interpretation from the list above.

a. Diabetic ketoacidosis.

b. A child suffering from acute asthma of moderate severity.

c. Low pH, normal PCO_2, normal pO_2, low bicarbonate.

d. Low pH, high PCO_2, normal pO_2, normal bicarbonate.

e. High pH, normal PCO_2, normal pO_2, high bicarbonate.

f. High pH, low PCO_2, normal pO_2, normal bicarbonate.

147 Biochemical abnormalities   PAED

Options
1 High sodium
2 Low sodium
3 High calcium
4 Low calcium
5 High chloride
6 Low chloride
7 High potassium

Questions
Identify the most likely biochemical abnormality in the following conditions.

a. Cystic fibrosis.

b. Syndrome of inappropriate antidiuretic hormone secretion.

c. Pyloric stenosis.

d. Dehydration.

e. The admission blood tests in a case of diabetic ketoacidosis.

148 Development   PAED

Options
1   Birth
2   6 weeks
3   4 months
4   6 months
5   9-10 months
6   12 months
7   15 months
8   18 months
9   3 years
10 4 years

Questions
At what age would you expect a child with normal development to be able to do the following?

a. Sit unsupported.

b. Have complete head lag.

c. Hold a rattle and shake purposefully.

d. Transfer objects from hand to hand.

e. Build a tower of three cubes.

f. Draw a circle.

149 Development PAED

Options
1. Birth
2. 6 weeks
3. 4 months
4. 6 months
5. 9-10 months
6. 12 months
7. 15 months
8. 18 months
9. 4 years
10. 5 years

Questions
At what age would you expect a child with normal development to be able to do the following?

a. Draw a triangle.

b. Draw a cross.

c. Immature pincer grasp.

d. Walk independently and stoop to pick up objects.

e. Maintain a standing position with support.

150 Social development   PAED

Options
1 6 weeks
2 16 weeks
3 6 months
4 9 -12 months
5 5 months
6 18 months
7 2.5 years
8 3 years

Questions
When would you expect a normal child to exhibit these stages of their development?

a. Dress themselves, except buttons.

b. Peek a boo and wave bye bye.

c. Laugh out loud.

d. Drink from a cup.

e. Spoon-feeding by themselves.

151 Vaccination   **PAED**

Options
1 Polio
2 Measles
3 Mumps
4 Rubella
5 Tuberculosis
6 Diphtheria
7 Tetanus
8 Pertussis
9 Meningococcus C
10 Haemophilus meningitis

Questions
Pick from the list above the most likely answer.

a. This was a major cause of meningitis before introduction of the vaccination in young children, the vaccination is a polysaccharide capsule of killed organism conjugated with protein. Only effective against type B infection.

b. This organism enters the body through open wounds. Its neurotoxin causes progressive painful muscle spasms. The vaccination is an inactivated toxin. A booster is required every 10 years.

c. This virus causes fever and enlargement of the parotid glands. Complications include sensorineural deafness and orchitis in adults.

d. This virus causes anterior horn cell damage leading to paralysis.

e. This virus causes the fetus to develop cataracts, deafness and congenital heart disease.

f. This organism causes a disease that is difficult to diagnose but the Heaf or Mantoux skin test may help.

152 Causes of shortness of breath   PAED

Options
1 Croup
2 Pneumonia
3 Bronchiolitis
4 Heart failure
5 Tuberculosis
6 Acute asthma
7 Viral-induced wheeze
8 Whooping cough
9 Inhaled foreign body

Questions
Pick the most likely clinical scenario.

a. A 3-year old boy who develops a barking cough and has some stridor.

b. A toddler with unilateral wheeze and shortness of breath.

c. A 8-year old Asian child who recently went to India, now has night sweats, loss of appetite, failure to thrive, and malaise.

d. A 13-year old girl with known ventral septal defect, now has ankle pitting oedema and bibasal crepitation in the lung fields.

e. A 1-year old child has coryzal symptoms followed by a cough and respiratory distress with a wheeze. A nasopharyngeal aspirate reveals presence of respiratory syncytial virus.

153 Diarrhoea   PAED

Options
1 Toddlers diarrhoea
2 Parasite
3 Cow's milk protein intolerance
4 Inflammatory bowel disease
5 Overflow diarrhoea
6 Secondary lactose intolerance
7 Coeliac disease
8 Cystic fibrosis
9 Non-specific diarrhoea

Questions
Pick the most likely clinical scenario in each of these patients with diarrhoea.

a. A 3 year-old child is failing to thrive and has a positive sweat test.

b. A child whose friend has recently had persistent diarrhoea.

c. An 8 year-old child has diarrhoea with blood and mucus. He has recently been losing weight.

d. A 2 year-old child has failure to thrive, is irritable, does not like food and has vomiting and diarrhoea. He has abdominal distension, wasted buttocks and is pale. The stools are pale and foul-smelling. The child also has finger clubbing.

e. A toddler has diarrhoea. He is drinking a lot of fluid. The child is growing normally.

154 Headache   PAED

Options
1 Tension headache
2 Eye strain
3 Migraine
4 Sinusitis
5 Dental disease
6 Space occupying lesion
7 Meningitis
8 Hypertension

Questions
Pick the most likely cause of headache.

a. A 13 year-old girl has poor oral hygiene and has not been taken to the dentist regularly.

b. A 14 year-old boy experiences fortification spectra followed by a severe headache which resolves with sleep.

c. A child has no concerning features on history or examination but is being bullied at school.

d. A 9 year-old girl presents with headache, high fever and has a capillary refill time of 3-4 seconds.

e. An 11 year-old girl presented with headache that is made worse by lying flat.

155 Leg pain and limp   PAED

Options
1 Growing Pains
2 Transient synovitis
3 Septic arthritis
4 Trauma
5 Osteomyelitis
6 Perthes disease
7 Slipped upper femoral epiphysis
8 Neoplastic disease

Questions
Pick the most likely condition.

a. A child who has leg pain, persistent fever and raised C-reactive protein (CRP) with no clear source identified on initial investigations.

b. A febrile child with hip pain, sickle cell disease, who is found to have *Salmonella* spp. positive blood cultures.

c. A 1 year-old boy with a minor respiratory tract infection develops a limp but has a normal physical examination and normal blood tests.

d. An overweight teenage boy, who has a gradual onset of pain in the groin. An X-ray confirms the diagnosis.

e. A 4-year old girl has pain at night, but no limp. The pain is in both arms and legs. The child is healthy. Examinations and investigations are normal. She is able to do all her normal activities.

156 Pyrexia   PAED

Options
1 Pneumonia
2 Hepatitis
3 Renal abscess
4 Dental abscess
5 Osteomyelitis
6 Infective endocarditis
7 Urinary tract infection
8 Gastro intestinal abscess
9 Infectious mononucleosis
10 Tuberculosis

Questions
Pick the most likely condition with these children with a temperature.

a. A boy has become unwell one month after a dental extraction and has splenomegaly on examination.

b. An 6 week-old is feeding poorly but there are no abnormalities on physical examination.

c. A teenager develops a morbilliform rash after you have prescribed amoxicillin for a sore throat a few days earlier.

d. A child recently returned from Africa presents with nausea and abdominal pain.

e. A 15 year-old with Crohn's disease thought to be suffering an exacerbation fails to respond to immunosuppresive treatment in hospital.

157 Heart murmurs

Options
1 Venous hum
2 Pulmonary flow murmur
3 Ejection systolic murmur
4 Aortic stenosis
5 Atrial septal defect
6 Pulmonary stenosis
7 Ventricular septal defect
8 Coarctation of the aorta
9 Innocent murmur

Questions
Pick from above the most likely cause.

a. Absent or delayed femoral pulses with a systolic murmur.

b. Harsh pansystolic murmur at lower left sternal border, radiating all over the chest.

c. Soft systolic murmur at the second left intercostal space with wide fixed splitting of the second sound.

d. Blowing continuous murmur in systole and diastole, heard below the clavicles and disappears on lying down.

e. Soft systolic ejection murmur at right upper sternal border, which radiates to neck and down left sternal border.

158 Anaemia   PAED

Options
1 Leukaemia
2 Renal failure
3 Chronic infection
4 Sickle cell disease
5 Lead poisoning
6 Thalassaemia trait
7 Iron deficiency anaemia

Questions
For each of the following scenarios, choose the most likely cause of anaemia from the list above.

a. A child with worsening school performance and abdominal pain.

b. High HbA2 and HbF on electrophoresis.

c. Low ferritin levels.

d. An afebrile child with a new onset limp.

e. A 9 month-old developing inconsolable crying whilst recovering from a bout of gastroenteritis.

159 Chromosomal abnormalities   PAED

Options
1 Trisomy 21
2 Trisomy 13
3 Trisomy 18
4 45 XO
5 Noonan syndrome
6 VACTERL syndrome
7 Pierre-Robin sequence

Questions
Match these syndromes with the chromosomal analysis.

a. Down's syndrome.

b. Edwards syndrome.

c. Turner syndrome.

d. Patau syndrome.

160 Neonatal jaundice   PAED

Options
1 Prematurity
2 Rhesus incompatibility
3 ABO incompatibility
4 Cystic fibrosis
5 Biliary atresia
6 TORCH
7 Hepatitis
8 Breast milk jaundice
9 Physiological
10 Bruising

Questions
For each scenario, identify the likely cause of the jaundice.

a. May cause ascites and pleural effusions in utero.

b. There is persistent jaundice with rising conjugated fraction. The child requires urgent surgical referral.

c. Conjugated hyperbilirubinaemia with thrombocytopenia.

161 Genetics

Options
1 Aneuploidy
2 Anticipation
3 Autosomal
4 Dominant
5 Empiric risk
6 Genotype
7 Homozygote
8 Gonadal mosaic
9 Duplication

Questions
Pick the best word corresponding to the definition below.

a. The occurrence of more than one genetic constitution of precursor cells of eggs or sperm.

b. Determined by a gene on one of the chromosomes other than the sex chromosomes.

c. The genetic constitution of an individual (either overall or referring to a specific gene locus).

d. An individual with identical alleles at the same locus.

e. Presence of an additional copy of part of a chromosome or of a gene.

162 Genetics   PAED

Options
1 Imprinting
2 Karyotype
3 Microdeletion
4 Monosomy
5 Penetrance
6 Phenotype
7 Recessive
8 Robertsonian translocation
9 Teratogen

Questions
Pick the best word corresponding to the definition below.

a. An agent which can damage the developing embryo.

b. A characteristic or disorder only expressed when both alleles at a genetic locus are altered.

c. The proportion of individuals with a particular genetic constitution which show its effect.

d. The absence of one member of a pair of chromosomes.

e. The chromosome constitution as displayed by a microscope.

f. The differential expression of a genetic characteristic or disease depending on parent of origin.

163 Skin infections   PAED

Options
1 Impetigo
2 Erythrasma
3 Staphylococcal scalded skin syndrome
4 Viral exanthema
5 Slapped cheek syndrome
6 Herpes simplex virus
7 Eczema herpeticum
8 Varicella zoster
9 Human papilloma virus
10 Molluscum contagiosum

Questions
Pick the most likely skin condition.

a. A common cutaneous infection of childhood caused by a pox virus.

b. This is caused by parvovirus B19.

c. This is responsible for 'viral warts'.

d. This is a highly infectious skin disease, presenting with typical honey coloured crust on the surface and is spread by direct contact.

e. This is frequently misdiagnosed as a fungal infection. It is caused by corynebacterium minutissimum.

164 Fungal infections   PAED

Options
1 Dermatophytes
2 Tinea corporis
3 Tinea cruris
4 Tinea pedis
5 Tinea capitis
6 Tinea incognito
7 Candida albicans
8 Pityrosporum

Questions
For each of the following, pick the most likely skin condition.

a. Ringworm of the groin.

b. Athlete's foot.

c. Ring worm of the scalp.

d. A term used to describe a fungal skin infection that has been modified by topical steroid.

e. This may cause a moist red rash with little satellite lesions in the nappy area of a child.

1400 EMQs for GPST/GPVTS entry

165 Neonatal skin conditions

PAED

Options

1 Strawberry naevus
2 Port-wine stain
3 Milia
4 Impetigo
5 Mongolian blue spot
6 Erythema toxicum
7 Acrodermatitis enteropathica
8 Giant congenital melanocytic naevi
9 Aplasia cutis congenita

Questions

For each of the following statements, pick the most likely skin condition from the list above.

a. Also known as capillary haemangioma.

b. Characterised by small keratin inclusion cysts.

c. A benign condition seen in 50% of Afro-Caribbean children.

d. A common transient blotchy maculopapular rash. The child is not toxic or unwell.

e. A rare congenital absence of skin usually over the scalp.

166 Childhood asthma   PAED

Options
1 Salbutamol as required
2 Montelukast sodium
3 Low-dose inhaled steroid
4 High-dose inhaled steroid
5 Oral steroid
6 Home salbutamol nebulisers
7 Long-acting beta-2 agonists
8 Change to a metered-dose inhaler

Questions
Pick the most appropriate next step in the management of the following asthmatic patients.

a. A 12-year-old boy currently using inhaled low-dose steroids and salbutamol approximately once weekly via spacer. He is increasingly independent and starting secondary school.

b. A 14-year-old keen netball player taking high-dose steroids and salbutamol. She finds her symptoms poorly controlled over the winter months and her sporting activities are limited by this.

c. A 4-year-old who rarely requires her salbutamol inhaler but has attended hospital twice already this winter with sudden exacerbations precipitated by viral illness.

d. An 8-year-old girl whose asthma is always exacerbated by a high pollen count and has been on high-dose inhaled steroids over the summer months, using her salbutamol once per fortnight.

167 Vitamins   PAED

Options
1 Vitamin K
2 Vitamin A
3 Vitamin D
4 Vitamin E
5 Folic Acid
6 Vitamin C
7 Vitamin B6

Questions
Of which of the above vitamins are each of the following statements true?

a. To maintain epithelial membranes and retinal pigment

b. For skin integrity and resistance to infection.

c. For normal red cell maturity.

d. Supplementation is required more frequently in children of African or Asian origin.

e. To prevent haemorrhagic disease of the newborn.

| 168 | Apgar score | PAED |

Options
1 0
2 1
3 2
4 3
5 4
6 5
7 6
8 7
9 8
10 10

Questions
Pick the Apgar score from above list.

a. Heart rate 80, irregular breathing, limp, no response to pharyngeal catheter, white baby.

b. Heart rate 120, no breathing, limp, grimacing, blue.

c. Heart rate 140, normal crying, active movements, cough, pink.

d. Heart rate 110, irregular breathing, diminished muscle tone, grimace, blue.

e. Heart rate 40, no breathing, limp, no response to pharyngeal catheter and white.

169 Statistics PAED

Options
1   Incidence
2   Prevalence
3   Mortality rate
4   Stillbirth rate
5   Perinatal mortality rate
6   Early neonatal mortality rate
7   Neonatal mortality rate
8   Postneonatal mortality rate
9   Infant mortality rate
10 Sensitivity

Questions
Which word best fits the definition below?

a. Infants born dead over 24 weeks' gestation per 1000 births.

b. Number of deaths between birth and 7th day of life per 1000 live births.

c. The proportion of a defined group having a disease at any one time.

d. Deaths up to 28 days of life per 1000 live births.

e. Number of deaths in infants under 1 year per 1000 live births.

170 Vaccinations   **PAED**

Options
  1 DTP
  2 Polio
  3 Hib
  4 Men C
  5 MMR
  6 BCG
  7 Tetanus
  8 Hepatitis B
  9 Pneumococcal

Questions
Pick the correct vaccine in view of the following statements.

  a. In some areas of the UK, it Is given to all shortly after birth.

  b. The oral form of this vaccine is no longer used routinely.

  c. Epiglottitis is now very rare since the introduction of this vaccine.

  d. The spores of this disease are present in the soil.

  e. This should be given to children without a functioning spleen.

171 Chromosomal abnormalities   PAED

Options
1 Klinefelter's syndrome
2 Turner's syndrome
3 Noonan's syndrome
4 Down's syndrome
5 Edwards syndrome
6 Patau's syndrome

Questions
For each of the following descriptions, match the most likely syndrome from the list above.

a. Overalapping fingers and macrocephaly.

b. Cleft lip, heart and eye defect.

c. Brushfield spots.

d. A male child with a heart defect and average intellect.

e. Shield chest and a trident hairline.

f. Pedal oedema in the neonatal period.

g. Slightly below average IQ and normal testicular size noted until puberty.

172 Cerebral palsy   PAED

Options
1 Nasogastric tube
2 Percutaneous endoscopic gastromy (PEG) tube
3 Baclofen
4 Botulinum injections
5 Mebeverine
6 Cetirizine patch
7 Hyoscine patch
8 Surgical loosening of the Achilles tendon
9 Ankle-foot orthosis

Questions
What would be the most appropriate management option for each of the following problems in a 10 year-old with cerebral palsy.

a. Excessive oral secretions.

b. Muscle spasms.

c. Severe muscle stiffness.

d. Recurrent aspiration with oral feeds.

e. Tightening of the Achilles tendon in hemiplegic cerebral palsy.

173 Adverse drug effects   **PAED**

Options
1 Staining of the teeth
2 Ototoxicity
3 Foetal limb defects
4 Renal failure
5 Drug-induced lupus
6 Heart failure
7 Purpura
8 Lung fibrosis
9 Haemorrhagic cystitis
10 Thrombosis

Questions
Choose the most well-recognised adverse effect of each of the following drugs.

a. Sulphonamides

b. Bleomycin

c. Tetracycline

d. Roaccutane® (retinol)

e. Cyclophosphamide

f. Gentamicin

174 Childhood epilepsy   PAED

Options
1 Absence seizures
2 Febrile convulsions
3 Rolandic epilepsy
4 Myoclonic epilepsy
5 Infantile spasms

Questions
Choose the most likely answer from the option list above.

a. The child stops what they are doing and stares into space.

b. May be confused with day dreaming.

c. Normal age for this to occur is 6 months to 5 years.

d. Clonic, partially sensorimotor attacks affect the face, bulbar muscles, hand and arm and are most common on waking.

e. Sudden involuntary spasm of a muscle or group of muscles. Consciousness is often maintained.

f. Runs of tonic spasms occur every 5-10 seconds. Most commonly are 'salaam' spasms.

175 Haematuria in children   PAED

Options
1 Acute glomerulonephritis
2 Benign recurrent haematuria
3 Haemolytic uraemic syndrome
4 Nephroblastoma
5 Renal venous thrombosis
6 Urinary tract infection
7 Non-accidental injury

Questions
For each of the following scenarios, pick the most likely diagnosis.

a. A 4 year-old child has an upper respiratory tract infection, followed 2 weeks later by haematuria associated with oliguria and periorbital oedema.

b. A 5 year-old boy presents with dark urine after recent severe gastroenteritis.

c. A 4 month-old child presents with an abdominal mass. Investigation shows a displacement of the right kidney and there is microscopic haematuria.

d. A 6 year-old has a number of episodes of painless macroscopic haematuria, with no evidence of a UTI and a normal IVU.

Pharmacology

176 Action of cardiology drugs   **PHARM**

Options
1 Aspirin
2 Clopidrogel
3 Streptokinase
4 Beta-blockers
5 Bisoprolol
6 Digoxin
7 Heparin
8 Warfarin
9 Tirofiban
10 Ramipril

Questions
For each of the following features, select the most likely drug.

a. Activates plasmin to degrade fibrin.

b. Interacts with the sodium potassium ATPase.

c. Is thought to act in part by cardiac remodelling.

d. Is a cyclo-oxygenase inhibitor.

e. Is an ADP-receptor antagonist.

177 Side effects of cardiology drugs **PHARM**

Options
1 Aspirin
2 Clopidrogel
3 tPA
4 Adenosine
5 Calcium channel blockers
6 Amiodarone
7 Atorvastatin
8 Enalapril

Questions
Match the side effects to the most likely drugs above.

a. Ankle swelling.

b. Bronchospasm.

c. Hyperthyroidism.

d. Alveolitis.

e. Rhabdomyolysis

f Cough.

178 Cardiovascular drug choices — PHARM

Options
1 Nimodipine
2 Lidocaine (Lignocaine)
3 Atropine
4 Nicorandil
5 Bendroflumethiazide (Bendrofluazide)
6 Furosemide (Frusemide)
7 Bumetanide
8 Losartan
9 Spironolactone
10 Isosorbide mononitrate

Questions
Choose the best drug for the following situations.

a. Bradycardia in a cardiac arrest.

b. A hypertensive patient who experiences an irritating cough due to your first option drug.

c. A patient with acute pulmonary oedema, who has already been given oxygen and opiates.

d. A seventy year-old patient with angina which fails to be controlled by buccal spray alone.

e. A patient suffering an acute subarachnoid haemorrhage.

179 Pharmacokinetics.   PHARM

Options
1 Induces liver enzymes to enhance the metabolism of other drugs
2 Inhibits liver enzymes and so reduces the metabolism of other drugs
3 Levels of this drug are affected by the action of liver enzymes

Questions
Each of the following drugs interacts with the liver. In which way do they principally interact?

a. Warfarin.

b. Combined oral contraceptive pill.

c. Phenytoin.

d. Rifampicin.

e. Clarithromycin.

180 Drug interactions.   **PHARM**

Options
1 Allopurinol
2 Alcohol
3 Monoaminoxydase inhibitors
4 ACE inhibitors
5 Digoxin
6 Levodopa
7 Lithium
8 Sildenafil (Viagra ®)
9 Statins
10 Diltiazem

Questions
With which drug do the following drugs interact to cause the following effects?

a. Fibrates – causing increased frequency of myopathy and rhabdomyolysis.

b. Tyramine – causing acute hypertensive crisis.

c. Beta blockers – enhanced hypotensive effect.

d. Metronidazole – causing nausea and vomitting.

e. Beta blockers – risk of bradychardia or asystole due to AV block.

f. Nicorandil – significant hypotensive effect.

g. Azathioprine – significant risk of bone marrow suppression.

181 Drugs and pregnancy   **PHARM**

Options
1 Tooth discolouration
2 Eight cranial nerve damage
3 General teratogenicity
4 Kernicterus
5 Foetal hypothyroidism
6 Foetal hypoglycaemia
7 Foetal and neonatal hypoglycaemia
8 Osteoporosis
9 No harmful effects reported
10 Arthropathy

Questions
What effect on the foetus may each the following drugs lead to?

a. Heparin.

b. Fluconazole.

c. Amiodarone.

d. Tetracycline.

e. Aminoglycosides.

f. Podophyllotoxin.

g. Cefotaxime

h. Trimethoprim.

182 Side effects of drugs   PHARM

Options
1 Osteopenia
2 Peripheral neuropathy
3 Anorgasmia
4 Neutropenia
5 Gum hypertrophy
6 Jaundice
7 Haemorrhagic cystitis
8 Convulsions

Questions
Which of the options above are characteristic side effects of each of the following drugs?

a. Phenytoin.

b. Carbimazole.

c. Clozapine.

d. Isoniazid.

e. Corticosteroids.

f. Cyclophosphamide.

g. Lignocaine.

h. Fluoxetine.

| 183 | Pain control | PHARM |

Options
1 Paracetamol
2 Epidural
3 Diamorphine
4 Amitriptyline
5 Ibuprofen
6 Diclofenac
7 Codydramol
8 Morphine sulphate tablets
9 Fentanyl lozenge

Questions
Out of the options above, which is the best drug for each of the following scenarios?

a. 40 year-old female with extensive metastatic breast carcinoma who is comfortable at rest but experiences intense pain moving from bed and undertaking physical activities.

b. 50 year-old male experiencing colicky pain due to large renal calculus.

c. 50 year-old woman, post-operative varicose vein avulsion and stripping.

d. 80 year-old with acute myocardial infarction.

e. 8 year-old with minor trauma after falling from bicycle.

f. 30 year-old male with post-herpetic neuralgia.

g. 85 year-old male from a nursing home with long-standing osteoarthritis.

184 Drug treatment for hypertension — PHARM

Options
1 Alpha blockers
2 ACE inhibitors
3 Angotensin II antagonists
4 Beta blockers
5 Calcium channel blockers
6 Thiazide diuretics

Questions
Choose the most likely drug in relation to the following statements.

a. May precipitate gout.

b. Can cause profound hypotension and so initially may be started in the evening time.

c. Postural hypotension is a common side effect.

d. Also used as a treatment for prostatism.

e. Avoid in patients with peripheral vascular disease.

f. May cause sleep disturbances.

185 Antiarrhythmics   PHARM

Options
1 Lidocaine (Lignocaine)
2 Digoxin
3 Verapamil
4 Sotalol
5 Flecainide
6 Amiodarone
7 Adenosine

Questions
Pick the most likely group of drugs.

a. Used to terminate supreaventricular tachycardias after failure of vagal manoeuvres.

b. Its actions are enhanced in hypokalaemia.

c. An example of a class IV antiarrhythmic.

d. Contraindicated in a patient with heart failure.

e. Contraindicated in Wolff-Parkinson-White syndrome and hypertrophic obstructive cardiomyopathy with sinus rhythm.

f. Causes a "slate grey" complexion in some patients.

g. A class III antiarrhythmic.

186 Diuretics   PHARM

Options
1 Loop diuretic
2 Thiazide diuretic
3 Carbonic anhydrase inhibitor
4 Potassium-sparing diuretic
5 Osmotic diuretic

Questions
Choose the most likely class of diuretic.

a. Inhibits the exchange of sodium for potassium ions in the distal tubule.

b. Amiloride is an example.

c. Mannitol is an example.

d. Acts on the distal tubule, where it inhibits the active transport of sodium ions.

e. Frusemide is an example.

f. Bumetanide is an example.

g. Spironolactone is an example.

187 Antidepressants   PHARM

Options
1 Tricyclic antidepressant
2 Selective serotonin reuptake inhibitor
3 Serotonin and noradrenaline reuptake inhibitor
4 Presynaptic alpha 2 antagonist
5 Monoamine oxidase inhibitor

Questions
Choose the correct class of antidepressant.

a. Marmite should be avoided.

b. Broad bean pods should be avoided.

c. Mirtazapine is an example.

d. Citalopram is an example.

e. Venlafaxine is an example.

f. Paroxetine is an example.

g. Strongly contraindicated post-myodardial infarction and in those with arrhythmias.

188 Neurodegenerative disease　　　　　　　PHARM

Options
1 Levodopa
2 Carbidopa
3 Selegiline
4 Entacapone
5 Bromocriptine
6 Benzatropine
7 Donepezil
8 Riluzole
9 Interferon beta 1a

Questions
Which drug is the most appropriate?

a. Used to slow the progression in some forms of motor neurone disease.

b. Can be used to reduce the frequency and severity of relapses in multiple sclerosis.

c. A monoamine oxydase-B inhibitor.

d. A dopamine receptor agonist used in refractory parkinsonism.

e. A catecholamine-O-methyltransferase (COMT) inhibitor used to improve symptom control in parkinsonism.

f. May improve some of the early symptoms of early dementia.

g. A peripheral decarboxylase inhibitor which reduces the peripheral side effects of levodopa.

189 Antibiotics   **PHARM**

Options
1. Penicillin
2. Cephalosporin
3. Monobactam
4. Tetracycline
5. Macrolide
6. Sulphonamide
7. Aminoglycoside
8. Metronidazole
9. Quinolone

Questions
Choose the most likely class of antibiotic.

a. Often first line agent for atypical pneumonias.

b. Ciprofloxacin is an example.

c. Resistance is classically by the acquisition of a beta lactimase.

d. Acts by inhibiting the enzyme DNA gyrase that is responsible for maintaining the structure of bacterial DNA.

e. Have ototoxic and nephrotoxic effects.

f. Used to treat conditions involving anaerobic bacteria.

| 190 | Drugs for urinary flow disorders | PHARM |

Options
1 Oxybutynin
2 Duloxetine
3 Collagen
4 Bethanechol chloride
5 Doxazosin
6 Finasteride

Questions
Match the most suitable remedy to the following statements.

a. This is a cholinergic used to treat urinary retention.

b. This is a 5-alpha reductase inhibitor used to treat benign prostatic hypertrophy (BPH).

c. This is used to treat women with stress incontinence.

d. This can be used to treat urge incontinence.

e. This blocks sympathetic activity to cause relaxation of the smooth muscle of the prostate and is used in BPH.

| 191 | Vitamins | PHARM |

Options

1 Vitamin A
2 Vitamin B$_1$
3 Vitamin B$_6$
4 Vitamin B$_{12}$
5 Vitamin C
6 Vitamin D
7 Vitamin E
8 Vitamin K
9 Multiple water-soluble vitamins

Questions

Which vitamin from the above list corresponds best to each of the following statements?

a. Is administered parenterally to alcoholics when admitted to hospital

b. Is administered to those with pernicious anaemia.

c. Asian women and housebound elderly may need supplementation of this vitamin.

d. Over-the-counter supplementation is contraindicated during pregnancy.

e. Is administered orally to prevent Wernicke's encephalopathy.

f. Deficiency is rare in the UK and supplementation is often indicated during anti-TB treatment.

g. High doses may lead to hypercalcaemia.

h. Is also known as hydroxocobalamin.

192 Coughs

Options
1. Antitussives
2. Expectorants
3. Decongestants
4. Sympathomimetics
5. Demulcents

Questions
Match the most suitable remedy to the following statements.

a. May reduce rhinorrhoea

b. Tend to be syrups which can coat surfaces to sooth and relieve dry irritating coughs.

c. Mucoletics are an example of this type of drug; they can reduce viscosity of bronchial secretions, thereby facilitating their removal.

d. Reduce the sensitivity of the cough centre.

e. Most of these are opiates and should be avoided in chronic obstructive airways disease.

193 Glaucoma   **PHARM**

Options

1 Miotics
2 Beta blockers
3 Alpha 2 agonists
4 Sympathomimetics
5 Carbonic anhydrase inhibitors
6 Prostaglandin analogues

Questions

All of the drugs listed above are used to reduce pressure in glaucoma.
Which drug is the most suitable for each of the following statements?

a. Increase uveoscleral outflow of the aqueous humour and may change eye colour.

b. Suppress production of aqueous humour.

c. Poorly tolerated by the young and by myopes.

d. Include drugs such as pilocarpine and carbachol.

e. Cause constriction of the ciliary muscle which helps to open the drainage channels in the trabecular meshwork between the iridocorneal junction and the canal of Schlemm.

f. Acetazolamide is an example.

| 194 | Psoriasis, seborrhoea, ichthyosis | PHARM |

Options
1 Dithranol
2 Coal tar
3 Cade oil
4 Topical steroids
5 Ciclosporin
6 Systemic retinoid
7 Topical retinoid
8 Vitamin D analogue
9 Ketoconazole
10 Topical lithium

Questions
Which of the above option best corresponds to each of the following statements?

a. Active against pityrosporum ovale, an organism implicated in seborrhoeic dermatitis of the scalp.

b. Contraceptive measures must be used by women during and for some time after treatment.

c. Stains skin and clothes heavily.

d. The mechanism of action is thought to be by suppression of T lymphocyte activity in the dermis and epidermis, thereby reducing epidermal hyperproliferation.

e. Roaccutane ® is an example.

195 Side effects   **PHARM**

Options
1 Amiodarone
2 Aspirin
3 Atenolol
4 Carbimazole
5 Chlorpromazine
6 Erythromycin
7 L-Dopa
8 Lisinopril
9 Lithium
10 Metformin

Questions
Pick the drug that is most likely for each of the following group of side effects.

a. Cold hands and feet, fatigue and impotence.

b. Peripheral neuropathy, pulmonary fibrosis, hyperthyroidism.

c. Postural hypotension, involuntary movements, nausea, discolouration of the urine.

d. Thirst, polyuria, tremor, rashes and hypothyroidism.

e. Sore throat, rash, nausea, pruritus.

196 Prescribing for patients with renal failure — PHARM

Options
1 No changes required
2 Reduced dose
3 Reduced dose frequency
4 Absolutely contraindicated
5 Relatively contraindicated
6 Higher doses may be needed
7 Drug levels must be monitored more often

Questions
Choose the best option for these drugs in renal failure.

a. Heparin in moderate renal impairment.

b. Gentamicin in chronic renal impairment.

c. Frusemide for pulmonary oedema in severe acute renal failure.

d. Phenytoin in severe renal impairment.

e. Cefalexin in severe chronic renal impairment.

197 Topical steroids potency   PHARM

Options
1 Mild
2 Moderate
3 Potent
4 Very potent

Questions
How potent are these steroids?

a. Betnovate.

b. Hydrocortisone 1%.

c. Dermovate.

d. Elocon.

e. Eumovate.

f. Fucibet.

198 Poisoning   PHARM

Options
1 Flumazenil
2 Activated charcoal
3 Sodium caclium edetate
4 Naloxone
5 N-Acetylcysteine
6 Atropine
7 Dicobalt edetate

Questions
What specific treatments are available for overdose of these substances?

a. Paracetamol

b. Opioids

c. Benzodiazepines

d. Heavy metals.

e. Organophosphates.

f. Carbamates.

g. Cyanide.

199 Diagnostic odours   PHARM

Options
1 Acetone
2 Acrid
3 Ammonia
4 Bitter almonds
5 Burnt rope
6 Rotten egg
7 Garlic
8 Mothballs

Questions
What do these drugs/poisons smell like?

a. Camphor.

b. Organophosphate.

c. Marijuana.

d. Cyanide.

e. Uraemia.

200 Adverse drug effects   PHARM

Options

1 Amiodarone
2 Amphotericin
3 Ampicillin
4 Bleomycin
5 Cyclosporin
6 Digoxin
7 Methotrexate
8 Phenytoin
9 Retinoids
10 Salbutamol

Questions

Which drug from the list above is most likely associated with each of the following side effects?

a. Gynaecomastia.

b. Severe mucositis.

c. Dry mucous membranes.

d. Fine tremor.

e. Hypertrichosis.

P Psychiatry

201 Examination of mental state   PSYCH

Options
1 Appearance and behaviour
2 Speech
3 Mood
4 Thinking
5 Perception
6 Cognitive function
7 Insight

Questions
Select the most appropriate category for each of the following elements of the mental state examination.

a. Usually lost in acute psychosis.

b. Counting backwards from twenty is used as part of its assessment.

c. Assessed types include: objective, subjective and congruity.

d. Delusions.

e. Sometimes doctors ask for the name of the Queen in this section.

202 Mental Health Act   PSYCH

Options
1 Section 3
2 Section 4
3 Section 5(2)
4 Section 5(4)
5 Section 20 (4)
6 Section 136
7 Section 135
8 Section 2

Questions
Which part of the Mental Health Act 1983 is relevant to the situations below?

a. Allows police to arrest a person 'in a place to which the public have access' and who is believed to be suffering from a mental disorder. The patient must be conveyed to a 'place of safety' for assessment by two doctor and an approved social worker.

b. This empowers an approved social worker who believes that someone is being ill-treated or is neglecting himself to apply to a magistrate to search for and admit such patients.

c. This is for a period of assessment (and treatment) lasting 28 days. An approved social worker (or nearest relative) makes the application on the advice of two doctors.

d. Any doctor may detain a patient, already admitted on a medical or psychiatric ward, who wishes to leave the hospital and has a mental illness placing them at risk of harming themselves or others for 72 hours whilst a further assessment is requested.

e. This permits a nurse to detain for 6 hours a patient (already admitted onto a ward) who has a mental illness currently putting them at risk of harming themselves or others and who wishes to leave the ward against advice.

203 Sociological concepts

Options
1 Social role
2 Sick role
3 Illness behaviour
4 Social class
5 Life event
6 Culture
7 Social mobility
8 Migration
9 Social institution
10 Total institution

Questions
Match up the most likely descriptive term.

a. Movement between societies.

b. A place where people spend all their time in one place and have little freedom to their way of life.

c. Behaviour expected and required of an ill person.

d. A change of role or status in a society.

e. The way of life shared by a group of human beings.

204 Personality disorders   PSYCH

Options
1 Anxious
2 Obsessive-compulsive
3 Dependent
4 Affective
5 Paranoid
6 Schizoid
7 Schiotypal
8 Histrionic
9 Borderline
10 Narcissistic

Questions
Which type of personality disorder best matches the description?

a. People with this disorder have unstable relationships, impulsivity, chronic feelings of emptiness, and variable moods.

b. Characterised by an abnormal sense of self-importance, and ideas of success, power and intellect superior to others.

c. These people are emotionally cold, self-sufficient, and detached. They are introspective and may have a complex fantasy life.

d. These people are passive and unduly compliant with the wishes of others. They lack vigour and self-reliance and they avoid responsibility.

e. Persons with this disorder are unduly focussed on unimportant details and are indecisive.

205 Mechanisms of defence   PSYCH

Options
1 Repression
2 Denial
3 Regression
4 Displacement
5 Projection
6 Reaction formation
7 Rationalisation
8 Sublimation
9 Identification

Questions
Which mechanism of defence is being described?

a. The unconscious diversion of unacceptable impulses into more acceptable outlets.

b. The unconsious adoption of behaviour opposite to that which would reflect true feelings and intentions.

c. A concept put forward to explain why people sometimes behave as if unaware of something of which they are in fact adequately informed.

d. The unconscious provision of a false but acceptable explanation for behaviour that has a less acceptable origin.

e. People behaving in a way more appropriate to an earlier stage of development.

206 Disorders of sexual preference   **PSYCH**

Options
1 Fetishism
2 Fetishistic transvestism
3 Paedophilia
4 Exhibitionism
5 Voyeurism
6 Sadomasochism

Questions
Pick the best option for each of the following definitions.

a. Sexual arousal is obtained by exposure of the genitalia to an unprepared stranger.

b. Observation of others as the preferred and repeated way of obtaining sexual arousal.

c. Preference for sexual activity that involves bondage or inflicting pain on another person.

d. Inanimate objects are the preferred or only means of achieving sexual excitement.

e. Repeatedly wearing clothes of the opposite sex as the preferred or only means of sexual arousal.

207 Causes of learning disability   PSYCH

Options
1 Triple X
2 Cri du chat
3 Phenylketonuria
4 Homocystinuria
5 Galactosaemia
6 Tay-Sachs disease
7 Hurler's syndrome
8 Lesch-Nyhan

Questions
Match the most suitable syndrome to the following aetiologies.

a. Autosomal recessive disorder resulting in increased lipid storage.

b. Autosomal recessive disorder with absence of cystathione synthetase.

c. Trisomy X.

d. Deletion in chromosome 5.

e. X-linked recessive disorder leading to enzyme defect affecting purine metabolism. Excessive uric acid production and excretion.

208 The Mental Health Act   **PSYCH**

Options
1 28 days
2 6 months
3 3 months
4 72 hours
5 48 hours
6 24 hours
7 6 hours

Questions
What is the duration available for detention in these orders?

a. Treatment order under Section 3.

b. Assessment order under Section 2.

c. Section 5 (2).

d. Section 5 (4).

e. Section 136.

209 Physical signs in psychiatry.   PSYCH

Options
1 Anorexia nervosa
2 Bulimia nervosa
3 Anxiety
4 Depression
5 Manic
6 Parkinsonian
7 Opiate intoxication
8 Opiate withdrawal
9 Thyrotoxicosis
10 Treated schizophrenia

Questions
To which of the above conditions are each of the following signs associated?

a. Russell's sign

b. Lanugo hair

c. Piloerection

d. Gynaecomastia

e. Parotid enlargement

f. Festinating gait

g. Pupil dilation

210 Culture-bound syndromes   PSYCH

Options
1. Dhat
2. Djinn
3. Gas
4. Koro
5. Latah
6. Shinkeishitus
7. Susto
8. Windigo

Questions
To which of the above syndromes do each of the following descriptions apply?

a. Hypersensitivity to sudden fright, with command obedience, echolalia, echopraxia and a trance-like state. It is seen in Malaysia and Indonesia.

b. The belief in possession by a genie.

c. The sudden intense fear of the penis shrinking into the abdomen and causing death, seen most often in men from South East Asia.

211 Benzodiazepines   PSYCH

Options
1 0.5 mg
2 1 mg
3 5 mg
4 10 mg
5 15 mg

Questions
What dosage of the following drugs is equivalent to 5 mg of diazepam?

a. Chlordiazepoxide.

b. Lorazepam.

c. Temazepam.

d. Nitrazepam.

212 Alcohol dependence syndrome   PSYCH

Options
1 Primacy
2 Compulsion
3 Stereotype
4 Tolerance
5 Relief
6 Withdrawal
7 Reinstatement

Questions
Which criteria of alcohol dependence syndrome is being described in each of the following statements?

a. There is an increase in the amount of alcohol required to achieve the effects originally produced by a lower amount.

b. A return to the original dependence type of drinking after a period of not drinking.

c. When alcohol is drunk to prevent withdrawal symptoms.

d. The drinking of alcohol takes precedence over all other activities.

e. Developing a pattern of drinking at a particular place or time.

213 Carbamazepine   PSYCH

Options
1 This drug is likely to increase carbamazepine levels
2 This drug is likely to decrease carbamazepine levels
3 The level of this drug is likely to be decreased by carbamazepine
4 The level of this drug is likely to be increased by carbamazepine
5 The level of this drug is likely to be unchanged by carbamazepine

Questions
For each of the following drugs, identify the most likely interaction with carbamazepine.

a. Cimetidine.

b. Haloperidol.

c. Oral contraceptives.

d. Phenytoin.

e. Phenobarbitone.

214 Behavioural therapies   PSYCH

Options
1 Systematic desensitisation
2 Aversive therapy
3 Token economy
4 Modelling
5 Flooding

Questions
Identify the behavioural treatment that is being described in each of the following statements.

a. Encouragement of activities and rewarding with credits that can be exchanged for gifts.

b. Disulfuram is a pharmacological treatment that may be used for this purpose.

c. A nasty stimulus occurs in order to stop the behaviour.

d. Based on a theory that observational learning encourages adaptive behaviour.

e. The patient is exposed to the feared object immediately.

215 Bizarre movements and postures   **PSYCH**

Options
1 Echopraxia
2 Ambitendency
3 Waxy flexibility
4 Phantom phenomena
5 Automatic obedience
6 Catatonic frenzy
7 Tics
8 Schnauzkraumpf
9 Parkinsonism

Questions
Identify the movement or posture being described in each statement.

a. Repetitive, irregular, jerky movements involving one or a collection of muscles.

b. Features include cogwheel rigidity, festinant gait, and resting tremor.

c. The patient sustains postures with no apparent distress for periods that are longer than would normally be managed without discomfort. The limbs may remain positioned where they are passively moved to.

d. Undirected, incessant, purposeless physical activity, which may appear as running in circles, turning round and round, or shaking the body while uttering bizarre sounds of excitement.

e. Imitative automatic repetition of movements, carried out by the patient despite requests to stop them.

216 Dementia   PSYCH

Options
1 Alcoholic dementia
2 Multi infarct dementia
3 Normal pressure hydrocephalus
4 Lewy body dementia
5 Alzheimer's disease
6 Parkinsonism
7 Huntington's chorea
8 Creutzfeldt-Jakob syndrome
9 Pseudodementia
10 Hypothyroidism

Questions
For each scenario, identify the most likely form of dementia.

a. An 82 year old with history of MI and strokes is getting increasingly confused and forgetful. His wife states that he has suddenly become a lot worse.

b. A 57-year old who has a pill-rolling tremor.

c. A 45-year old woman with myoclonic jerks, aphasia and primitive reflexes.

d. An 88 year old whose forgetfulness and confusion greatly improves with mirtazapine.

e. A 55 year old man sees you in a GP surgery complaining of tiredness, confusion, weight gain and low mood. On examination you notice he is pale, confused and speaks with a croaky voice.

Renal Medicine

217 Urinary tract investigations   **RENAL**

Options

1 Plain abdominal film
2 Plain abdominal radiograph
3 Intravenous urogram/pyelogram
4 Micturating cystourethrogram
5 Retrograde pyelogram
6 Renal arteriography
7 Isotope renal scans
8 Percutaneous nephrostomy
9 Magnetic resonance angiography

Questions

To which of the investigations above do each of the following statements refer?

a. This can reveal ureteric reflux when the patient is urinating.

b. Information obtained from this investigation includes: split renal function & uptake and excretory patterns of each kidney.

c. MAG 3 is an example.

d. An invasive imaging method used to locate obstructions within the urinary tract.

e. A useful non-invasive method of imaging renal artery stenosis.

218 Glomerular disease   **RENAL**

Options
1 Minimal change glomerulonephritis
2 Membranous glomerulonephritis
3 Focal segmental glomerulosclerosis
4 Membranoproliferative glomerulonephritis
5 Proliferative glomerulonephritis
6 Berger's disease
7 Rapidly progressive glomerulonephritis

Questions
Which type of glomerular disease do the following statements refer to?

a. Classically seen two weeks after a streptococcal infection.

b. Also called IgA disease, this is a common cause of recurrent haematuria in young men.

c. The basement membrane of the glomerulus appears split under a light microscope, resembling 'tram tracks'. It is associated with mixed essential cryoglobulinaemia and partial lipodystrophy.

d. Typically affects a child presenting with nephrotic syndrome.

e. Associated with Hodgkin's disease.

f. Also called mesangiocapillary glomerulonephritis.

219 Renal diseases   **RENAL**

Options
1 Acute nephritic syndrome
2 Interstitial nephritis
3 Myoglobinuria
4 Adult polycystic kidney disease
5 Medullary sponge kidney
6 Nephrocalcinosis
7 Nephrolithiasis
8 Diabetic nephropathy
9 Haemolytic-uraemic syndrome

Questions
Match the most suitable renal disease to the each of the following statements.

a. Occurs in rhabdomyolysis.

b. Kimmelstiel-Wilson lesions may be present and ACE inhibitors reduce microalbuminuria.

c. There is dilatation of renal collecting tubules.

d. Hyperparathyroidism and distal renal tubular acidosis are causes.

e. Characterised by a microangiopathic haemolytic anaemia, thrombocytopenia, fever and acute renal failure

f. An autosomal dominant condition (genes on chromosome 16 and 4)

g. Associated with aneurysms of intracerebral arteries.

220 Renal tubular disease   RENAL

Options
1 Renal tubular acidosis
2 Fanconi syndrome
3 Alport's syndrome
4 Hyperoxaluria
5 Cystinuria

Questions
Which renal tubular disease do the following statements refer to?

a. This hereditary nephritis is associated with sensorineural deafness, eye lesions and platelet dysfunction.

b. This involves a multiple proximal tubular defects leading to glycosuria, aminoaciduria, phosphaturia and renal tubular acidosis.

c. Types 1,2 and 4 exist.

d. This is the commonest cause of aminoaciduria.

221 Investigation for urinary tract symptoms   RENAL

Options
1 Urine microscopy and culture
2 Kidney, ureter and bladder (KUB) radiograph
3 Renal tract ultrasound
4 Urine cytology
5 Flexible cystoscopy
6 Barium enema
7 Prostate specific antigen
8 Blood glucose
9 Serum calcium
10 Urethral swab for microscopy and culture

Questions
Which is likely to be the most useful diagnostic test in the following scenarios?

a. A 21 year old man describes a three day history of urethral discomfort with a yellow discharge from his penis.

b. A 65 year old man complains of thirst, urinary frequency, fatigue and weight loss of one stone over the last three months.

c. A 58 year old tyre factory worker has noted a number of episodes of frank, painless haematuria but otherwise feels well.

d. A 65 year old woman presents with a short history of passing foul urine with green-brown discolouration. She has also noticed bubbles in her stream of urine. She has been treated for cervical carcinoma in the past.

222 Urinary incontinence   RENAL

Options
1 Urge incontinence
2 Stress incontinence
3 True incontinence
4 Retention with overflow
5 Urethral syndrome
6 Urinary tract infection
7 None of the above

Questions
In each of the following scenarios, what is the most likely diagnosis?

a. May be caused by faecal impaction.

b. A 65 year-old woman presents with urinary frequency. She experiences urinary incontinence as soon as the sensation to pass urine is felt.

c. A 65 year-old woman complains of repeatedly leaking small amounts of urine. This has occurred ever since she was treated for endometrial carcinoma.

d. A 65 year-old woman has noticed she leaks a small amount of urine every time she laughs, coughs or sneezes.

e. A 30-year woman complains of episodes of frequency, urgency and dysuria following sexual intercourse. Repeated mid-stream urine cultures are negative.

R Respiratory Medicine

223 Inhaler brand names   **RESP**

Options
1 Sodium chromoglycate
2 Terbulaline
3 Salmeterol
4 Tiotropium bromide
5 Ipratropium bromide
6 Beclometasone
7 Budesonide
8 Fluticasone
9 Fluticasone plus salmeterol

Questions
Match each of the following brand names to the correct inhaled drug.

a. Seretide®

b. Serevent®

c. Bricanyl®

d. Qvar®

e. Intal®

f. Pulmicort®

g. Spiriva®

224 Pathology RESP

Options
1 Chronic bronchitis
2 Emphysema
3 Asthma
4 Cor pulmonale
5 Bronchiectasis

Questions
For each of the following statements, determine the most appropriate pathology.

a. Reversible airway obstruction.

b. The development of pulmonary hypertension with subsequent secondary polycythaemia and right ventricular strain.

c. The production of sputum on most days for three months during any two consecutive years.

d. Destruction of the alveolar walls leads to permanent enlargement of the airways distal to the terminal bronchioles.

e. Permanent dilatation of the sub-segmental airways.

225 Impact of COPD   RESP

Options
1 25,000
2 100,000
3 1.5 million
4 15 million
5 22 million
6 100 million

Questions
What is the correct answer?

a. The mortality due to COPD in deaths per year in England and Wales.

b. The number of working days lost to COPD per year.

c. The yearly cost to the NHS in pounds per year.

d. The prevalence of COPD in the UK.

226 Lung function tests   RESP

Options
1 Slow vital capacity
2 Forced vital capacity (FVC)
3 Forced expiratory volume in one second (FEV_1)
4 The ratio of forced expiratory volume in one second over forced vital capacity (FEV_1/FVC)
5 Tidal volume
6 Residual volume

Questions
In each of the following statements, what is the parameter being referred to?

a. The total volume of air exhaled from a position of maximum inhalation to maximum exhalation using maximum effort.

b. The total volume of air exhaled in a relaxed manner from a position of maximum inhalation to maximum exhalation.

c. The volume of air exhaled in the first second of an exhalation from maximum inhalation using maximum effort.

d. Is reduced to less than 75% in those with obstructive airways disease.

227 Supporting smoking cessation   **RESP**

Options
1 Maintenance
2 Relapse
3 Contemplation
4 Action
5 Preparation
6 Pre-contemplation

Questions
Choose the best term to define the following stages smokers may go through to stop smoking.

a. They will consider stopping smoking but are not yet ready to do anything active about stopping.

b. They have managed not to smoke for 6 months or more.

c. They have stopped smoking, but are in the early (less than 6 months) stage of being a non-smoker.

d. Occasional lapses on the road to becoming a long-term quitter are normal and should be expected.

e. They do not intend to stop smoking in the near future and they may not perceive smoking to be a problem.

228 Drug therapy   RESP

Options
1 Short acting inhaled β_2 agonists
2 Short acting inhaled anticholinergics
3 Long acting inhaled β_2 agonists
4 Long acting inhaled anticholinergics
5 Oral β_2 agonists
6 Oral theophylline

Questions
For each of the following statements, pick the best option.

a. Tiotropium bromide is an example.

b. Can be used as an alternative for patients who are intolerant/unable to use other medications or as an add-on therapy.

c. Are used 3-4 times a day and the commonest side effect is a dry mouth.

d. Regular use can affect potassium levels.

e. Are used as needed and stimulate receptors in areas on the airway smooth muscle.

229 Lung diseases   **RESP**

Options
1 Chronic asthma
2 Chronic obstructive pulmonary disease
3 Bronchiectasis
4 Cystic fibrosis
5 Pulmonary fibrosis
6 Extrinsic allergic alveolits
7 Occupational lung disease
8 Granulomatous lung disease
9 Alpha-1-antitrypsin deficiency

Questions
For each of the following statements, match the most likely lung disease.

a. Has an autosomal recessive inheritance and 1 in 25 adults are carriers.

b. Kartagener's syndrome may be a cause.

c. This is a chronic inflammatory condition with variable airflow obstruction.

d. Amiodarone is a cause.

e. Almost all men with this condition are infertile.

f. Clinical features are dry cough, breathlessness, clubbing, cyanosis, fine late inspiratory creptitations.

g. IgG mediated type III hypersensitivity reaction to inhaled particles.

h. Silicosis is an example.

230 British Thoracic Society (BTS) "step guidelines" for asthma   **RESP**

Options

1 Step 1
2 Step 2
3 Step 3
4 Step 4
5 Step 5

Questions

For each of the scenarios below, which step is the patient currently treated on? You may assume that he/she is also taking the correct medication from lower steps.

a. Inhaled short acting β_2 agonists as required plus regular standard dose inhaled steroids.

b. A course of oral steroids in addition to a patient's usual medications.

c. Regular standard dose inhaled steroids plus a regular inhaled long acting β_2 agonist.

d. Regular medium dose inhaled steroid plus a regular inhaled long acting β_2 agonist.

e. Inhaled short acting β_2 agonists as required.

f. Regular high dose inhaled steroid plus a regular inhaled long acting β_2 agonist plus oral theophylline.

231 Occupational lung disease   RESP

Options
1. Coal worker's pneumoconiosis
2. Silicosis
3. Byssinosis
4. Berylliosis
5. Baritosis
6. Siderosis
7. Stannosis
8. Asbestosis

Questions
Which lung disease do the following statements relate to?

a. Caplan's syndrome may develop in patients with rheumatoid arthritis

b. Produces pleural plaques.

c. May affect quarry workers, stonemasons and hard rock miners.

d. Accounts for 90% of all compensated industrial lung disease.

e. Affects workers in cotton mills.

232 Shortness of breath   RESP

Options
1 Consolidation
2 Pneumothorax
3 Pleural effusion
4 Atelectasis
5 Bronchospasm
6 Fibrosis
7 Emphysema

Questions
You see a patient who is short of breath. Pick the most likely diagnosis to match these physical findings.

a. Unilateral reduced chest expansion, reduced vocal fremitus, stony dullness on percussion and absent breath sounds over a localised region with pleural rub above this region.

b. Unilateral reduced chest expansion, increased vocal fremitus, dullness on percussion and bronchial breathing.

c. Unilateral reduced chest expansion, reduced vocal fremitus and hyperresonance on percussion.

d. Bilateral reduced chest expansion, reduced vocal fremitus and hyperresonance to percussion.

233 Chest radiographs   RESP

Options
1. Neoplasm
2. Tuberculosis
3. Rib fracture
4. Sarcoidosis
5. Pleural effusion
6. Rheumatoid nodule
7. Pneumonia
8. Pulmonary embolus

Questions
For each statement, pick the most likely diagnosis.

a. A unilateral spiculated mass with bulky ipsilateral hilar lymphadenopathy

b. Upper lobe consolidation and cavitation in a 30 year-old Eastern European male who has haemoptysis.

c. On examination, a patient has bilateral stony dullness to percussion at both bases and the chest radiograph shows blunting of both costophrenic angles.

d. Bilateral hilar lymphadenopathy with bilateral pulmonary infiltrates.

234 Investigations   RESP

Options
1 Chronic obstructive pulmonary disease (COPD)
2 Asthma
3 Pulmonary embolus
4 Bronchiectasis
5 Lung carcinoma
6 Pleural effusion
7 Pneumothorax

Questions
For which of the conditions above are each of the following the best diagnostic test?

a. Spirometry.

b. High resolution CT thorax

c. Ventilation perfusion scan.

d. Mediastinoscopy may help in the management of this condition.

e. Serial peak flow measurements.

235 Haemoptysis

RESP

Options
1 Pulmonary tuberculosis
2 Bronchial carcinoma
3 Oesophageal varices
4 Bronchiectasis
5 Pulmonary embolism
6 Haemophilia
7 Goodpasture's syndrome

Questions
Pick the most suitable option for each of the statements below.

a. Is not a recognised cause of true haemoptysis.

b. Lead to haematemesis.

c. May also present with acute renal failure.

d. Pregnancy is a risk factor.

e. Excess alcohol consumption is a risk factor.

236 Inhaler devices

Options
1 Pressurised metered dose inhalers
2 Breath activated metered dose inhalers
3 Dry powder inhaler

Questions
What types of devices are used with these brands of inhalers?

a. Handihaler®

b. Easi-breathe®

c. Autohaler®

d. Accuhaler®

e. Evohaler®

f. Turbohaler®

g. Clickhaler®

S Rheumatology

237 Acute arthritis   RHEUM

Options
1 Septic arthritis
2 Gout
3 Pseudogout
4 Rheumatoid arthritis
5 Osteoarthritis
6 Acute sarcoidosis

Questions
Which acute arthritic disease is the most likely?

a. Lesch-Nyhan syndrome is a cause.

b. Causative organisms would include *Staphylococcus aureus.*

c. Polarised light microscopy of joint fluid reveals negatively birefringent needle-shaped crystals.

d. Most commonly affects first metatarsophalangeal joint.

e. Weakly positively birefringent crystals are present.

f. On examination there is a symmetrical deforming polyarthropathy involving the metacarpophalangeal, proximal interphalangeal and wrist joints with sparing of the distal interphalangeal joints.

238 Seronegative spondyloarthropathies   RHEUM

Options
1 Ankylosing spondylitis
2 Enteropathic spondyloarthropathies
3 Systemic lupus erythematosus (SLE)
4 Reiter's syndrome
5 Systemic sclerosis
6 Psoriatic arthritis

Questions
Pick the most likely disease for each of the following statements.

a. Can cause arthritis mutilans.

b. A young man who has recently been treated for non-specific urethritis presents with an acutely hot, swollen knee.

c. A young man presents with progressive lower back pain and stiffness with loss of lumbar lordosis.

d. May be associated with circinate balanitis, plantar fasciitis or keratoderma blenorrhagica.

e. Exercise, physiotherapy and non-steroidal anti-inflammatory drugs are the mainstay of treatment.

239	Connective tissue disorders and other seronegative arthropathies	RHEUM

Options

1 Systemic sclerosis
2 Mixed connective tissue disease
3 Polymyositis
4 Systemic lupus erythematosus (SLE)
5 Antiphospholipid syndrome
6 Juvenile idiopathic arthritis
7 Raynaud's phenomenon

Questions

Pick the most likely disease for each of the following statements.

a. In response to the cold, digits turn white and numb, then blue and cyanosed before finally turning red, painful and hyperaemic.

b. The limited cutaneous form of this disease includes the symptoms described with the old term 'CREST syndrome'. Skin involvement does not extend below the neck or proximally beyond the elbows or knees.

c. Predisposes to recurrent miscarriages.

d. Onset occurs before the age of 16.

e. The systemic form was formally known as Still's disease.

240 Autoantibodies in connective tissue disease   RHEUM

Options
1 Drug-induced lupus
2 Sjorgen's
3 Polymyositis
4 Diffuse cutaneous systemic sclerosis
5 Limited cutaneous systemic sclerosis
6 Antiphospholipid antibody syndrome
7 Mixed connective tissue disease

Questions
In which diseases do these autoantibodies normally occur?

a. Anticardiolipin.

b. Anti-ribonuclear protein (RNP)

c. Anti-Ro.

d. Anti-La.

e. Antihistones.

f. Anti-centromere

241 Neck problems RHEUM

Options
1 Spasmodic torticollis
2 Cervical spondylosis
3 Nerve root irritation or entrapment
4 Cervical rib
5 Whiplash injuries

Questions
Which neck problems do the following statements relate to?

a. Can cause thoracic outlet syndrome with pain and parasthaesia in the forearm and hand.

b. Neck pain due to stretching or tearing of cervical muscles and ligaments due to sudden, forced hyperextension of the neck.

c. Also known as 'wry neck'.

d. Sudden onset of a painful, stiff neck due to spasm of the trapezius and sternocleidomastoid muscles.

242 Shoulder problems   RHEUM

Options
1 Rotator cuff injury
2 Frozen shoulder
3 Acromioclavicular joint problems
4 Rupture of the long head of the biceps
5 Shoulder dislocation

Questions
Pick the shoulder problem that matches most loosely the following statements.

a. Also called adhesive capsulitis

b. A partial injury will cause a painful arc on examination.

c. On examination the shoulder contour is lost and there is flattening of the deltoid. The head of the humerus is seen as an anterior bulge.

d. On examination, there may be loss of sensation in a small patch below the shoulder.

e. Discomfort in the arm on lifting and feeling of 'something going'.

243 Elbow, wrist and hand problems   RHEUM

Options

1 Tennis elbow
2 Pulled elbow
3 Olecranon bursitis
4 Ulnar neuritis
5 Tenosynovitis
6 Golfers elbow
7 Dislocated elbow
8 Carpal tunnel syndrome
9 Ganglion
10 Trigger finger

Questions

Which condition do the following statements apply to?

a. A patient may notice increased clumsiness of the hand, with pain and numbness in the little finger and medial half of the ring finger.

b. Usually occurs due to a fall on an outstretched hand with a flexed elbow.

c. Finger in the fixed flexion position needs to be flicked straight by the other hand.

d. Tenderness over the lateral epicondyle and pain on resisted wrist extension.

e. Tenderness over the medial epicondyle and pain on resisted wrist pronation.

244 Knee problems   RHEUM

Options
1   Osteoarthritis of the knee
2   Infection of knee joint
3   Chondromalacia patella
4   Osgood-schlatter disease
5   Baker's cyst
6   Hypermobility
7   Patellar dislocation
8   Bipartite patella
9   Patella tendinitis
10 Burstitis

Questions
For each of the following, choose the most likely condition

a. An athletic teenager complains of episodes of knee pain following exercise, associated with a tender lump over the tibial tuberosity.

b. A teenage girl has symptoms of anterior knee pain when walking up and down the stairs.

c. May be an incidental radiographic finding but can cause tenderness if there is excessive mobility of the patella fragment.

d. Excessive kneeling is a risk factor for this condition

e. This may mimic a deep vein thrombosis on rupturing.

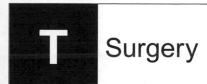

Surgery

245 Preoperative assessment   SURG

Options
1 Chest X-ray
2 ECG
3 Stress ECG
4 Nuclear medicine scan
5 Echocardiography
6 Coronary angiography
7 Peak flow rate
8 Spirometry

Questions
Which of the tests above is most likely described in each of the following statements?

a. Detects abnormalities of ventricular wall and assesses murmurs.

b. A useful screening test to detect cardiomegaly.

c. Shows the degree and extent of coronary occlusion.

d. A dynamic investigation which can suggest coronary ischaemia.

e. Can show venous congestion associated with cardiac failure.

246 Acute abdominal pain   SURG

Options
1 Appendicitis
2 Cholecystitis
3 Pancreatitis
4 Gastric perforation
5 Meckel's diverticulitis
6 Ulcerative colitis
7 Ischaemic bowel
8 Ruptured abdominal aortic aneurysm
9 Ruptured ovarian cyst
10 Ureteric obstruction, renal colic

Questions
For each statement, which is the most likely condition from the list above?

a. Uveitis is associated with this condition.

b. The two most common risk factors are gallstones and alcohol consumption.

c. The presentation is classically of nausea, anorexia and central abdominal pain localising to right iliac fossa.

d. Ranson's criteria help determine prognosis.

e. May present with bloody diarrhoea and shock in elderly patients with atrial fibrillation.

f. May be precipitated by high dose corticosteroid therapy.

g. A high serum lactate is helpful in suggesting this diagnosis.

h. Presentation may include acute renal impairment and loss of distal leg pulses

247 Hernias   **SURG**

Options
1 Hiatus hernia
2 Direct inguinal hernia
3 Indirect inguinal hernia
4 Femoral hernia
5 Exomphalos
6 Congenital umbilical hernia
7 Para umbilical hernia
8 Ventral hernia
9 Incisional hernia
10 Richter's hernia

Questions
Which type of hernia is being described?

a. This is herniation through the inguinal canal via the deep inguinal ring.

b. This is a rare condition in or part of the midgut remains exterior to the abdominal cavity during foetal maturity.

c. The herniation lies medial and inferior to the inguinal ligament.

d. This is divarication of the recti.

e. This hernia arises with part of the intestinal wall becoming incarcerated in the neck of the hernial sack.

248 Grading of haemorrhoids   SURG

Options
1 Grade 1
2 Grade 2
3 Grade 3
4 Grade 4

Questions
Allocate the correct grade to the following:

a. Haemorrhoidal lesions that prolapse via the anal canal on defaecation and require manual effort to reduce.

b. Swollen, tender anal cushions that do not exit the anal canal.

c. Lesions that descend from the anal canal on defaecation but reduce spontaneously.

d. Anal cushions that are permanently prolapsed out of the anal canal

249 Peripheral nerve injuries   **SURG**

Options
  1 Ulnar nerve
  2 Cervical sympathetic chain
  3 Median nerve
  4 Nerve roots C5 and C6
  5 Nerve roots C7, C8 and T1
  6 Long thoracic nerve of Bell
  7 Suprascapular nerve
  8 Musculocutaneous nerve
  9 Thoracodorsal nerve
10 Radial nerve

Questions
Which of the options above are most likely suited to each of the statements below?

a. Injury causes paralysis of serratus anterior muscle.

b. Injury causes weak shoulder abduction and external rotation.

c. Injury results in Erb's palsy.

d. Interruption leads to Horner's syndrome.

e. Clinical features of interruption are meiosis, ptosis, vasodilatation and anhidrosis of the face.

f. Guttering between the extensor tendon on the hand is noted with injury to this nerve.

250 Peripheral nerves   SURG

Options
1 Saphenous nerve
2 Common peroneal nerve
3 Sural nerve
4 Tibial nerve
5 Lateral cutaneous nerve of thigh
6 Sciatic nerve
7 Femoral nerve
8 Median nerve
9 Ulnar nerve
10 Radial nerve

Questions
Choose the most likely answer

a. The use of under-arm crutches may cause damage to this nerve.

b. Injury to this nerve will lead to loss of thumb adduction and a positive Froment's sign.

c. Compression causes carpal tunnel syndrome.

d. Proximal injury of the nerve leads to paralysis of ankle plantar flexion and sensory loss over the sole and calf.

e. Injury leads to foot drop and sensory loss over dorsum of foot.

251 Small bowel disease   SURG

Options
1 Intususseption
2 Crohn's disease
3 Mesenteric ischaemia
4 Small bowel tuberculosis
5 Strangulated hernia
6 Radiation enteritis
7 Meckel's diverticulum
8 Tumour at ampulla of Vater

Questions
Pick the most likely condition for each of the statements below.

a. May lead to stricture formation and malabsorption.

b. Can present with obstructive jaundice.

c. Causes spread of infection via Peyer's patches.

d. A rare cause of peptic ulceration beyond the duodenum.

e. A common cause of small bowel obstruction.

252	Large bowel disease	SURG

Options

1 Appendicitis
2 Carcinoma of the colon
3 Diverticular disease
4 Ulcerative colitis
5 Crohn's colitis
6 Angiodysplasia
7 Infective colitis

Questions

Pick the best option

a. Is associated with a history of constipation over many years.

b. Pseudopolyps can be found on colonoscopy.

c. A red cell scan during acute symptoms may aid diagnosis.

d. A barium enema study may reveal an "apple core" lesion.

e. Familial polyposis coli is a risk factor.

253 Conditions around the anus   SURG

Options
1 Perianal haematoma
2 Haemorrhoids
3 Anal fissure
4 Pilonidal sinus
5 Carcinoma of the anal canal
6 Rectal prolapse
7 Faecal incontinence
8 Faecal impaction

Questions
For each of the stems below, pick the best option from the list above.

a. This results from the ingrowth of hairs commonly in the postnatal cleft.

b. This presents as a small, often tender, dusky coloured swelling at the anal margin.

c. The patient may complain of painful defecation and may notice small amounts of fresh blood on toilet tissue after wiping.

d. Band ligation or injection therapy sclerotherapy are treatments.

e. This is an ulcer at the mucocutaneous junction between the anal canal and the rectum.

254	Thyroid cancer	SURG

Options
1 Papillary
2 Follicular
3 Medullary
4 Anaplastic

Questions
Pick the most appropriate type of thyroid cancer for each of the statements below.

a. It is associated with the MEN type 2 syndrome.

b. This has the worst prognosis.

c. This has the best prognosis.

d. This is the most common.

e. This develops from the calcitonin-secreting parafollicular cells.

255 Surgical complications — **SURG**

Options
1 Wound infection
2 Wound dehiscence
3 Fistula
4 Urinary tract infection
5 Subphrenic abscess
6 Compartment syndrome
7 Reflex sympathic dystrophy
8 Atelectasis
9 Myocardial infarction

Questions
Select the most likely surgical complication for each of the statements below.

a. Symptoms include a swinging pyrexia, nausea and abdominal pain radiating to the shoulder tip.

b. This can be treated by fasciotomy.

c. An abnormal communication forms between two epithelial line surfaces.

d. The rupture or splitting open of an anastomosis.

e. This can be prevented by early mobilisation and physiotherapy with breathing exercises.

f. The patient may complain of dysaesthesia, discoloration and abnormal sweating function on an area of skin.

256 Shortness of breath and general surgery   SURG

Options
1 Bronchopneumonia
2 Pulmonary embolism
3 Adult respiratory distress syndrome
4 Pneumothorax
5 Gastric aspiration
6 Pulmonary oedema
7 Hyperventilation
9 Tietze's syndrome
10 Dissecting aortic aneurysm

Questions
For each of the following statements, select amongst the options above the most likely diagnosis of these patients shortness of breath after an operation?

a. An 80 year-old lady nil by mouth following a bowel resection. She has a raised jugular venous pressure, sacral oedema and widespread crepitations on oscultation of the chest.

b. A 40 year-old woman has inadequate post-operative analgesia following an incisional hernia repair. She has poor air entry and a dull percussion note at her right lung base.

c. A 25 year-old female with a BMI of 30, who underwent emergency surgery for a rupture appendix. She became suddenly short of breath, tachicardic and hypotensive.

d. A 60 year-old man who suddenly became short of breath following insertion of a central venous catheter.

e. A 30 year-old alcoholic with epigastric pain and an amylase greater than 5000 becomes steadily more hypoxic, requiring intensive care support.

f. A 40 year-old woman who is operated on as an emergency following a road traffic accident. Intubation was difficult and a laryngeal mark was used. Postoperatively she is unwell and short of breath.

257 Lumps in the groin

SURG

Options
1. Hernia
2. Lymph nodes
3. Saphena varix
4. Psoas abscess
5. Psoas bursa
6. Femoral aneurysm
7. Hydrocele of a femoral hernia sac
8. Hydrocele of the cord
9. Ectopic testis

Questions
What is the most likely diagnosis for each of the following?

a. A soft compressible structure that is non-pulsatile, yet a bruit can be detected on oscultation.

b. If detected, distal trophic changes and peripheral pulses should be sought.

c. Elephantiasis of the limb occurs following disruption to this structure.

d. A collection of fluid to a congenital anomaly following the abnormal evolution of the tunica vaginalis.

258 Causes of a mass in the right iliac fossa   SURG

Options
1 Appendix mass
2 Appendix abscess
3 Tuberculosis
4 Carcinoma of the caecum
5 Crohn's disease
6 Iliac lymph nodes
7 Iliac artery aneurysm
8 Psoas abscess
9 Chrondroma of the ilium
10 Actinomycosis

Questions
Pick the most likely diagnosis for the following statements.

a. A large, hard, non tender structure that is fixed to the skeleton.

b. A middle-aged man presents with a six-month history of altered bowel habit, weight loss of 3kg and is anaemic. There is a palpable mass in the right lower quadrant on examination.

c. The patient will have been ill for several months with night sweats and loss of weight. There may also be back pain. The iliac fossa is filled with a soft, tender, dull, compressible mass. Pain is induced on flexion of the hip.

d. The patient has a history of righ iliac fossal pain and temperature settling with conservative management. He now represents with a period of central abdominal pain which then moves to the right iliac fossa. He has fever, malaise and poor appetite.

e. The patient complains of a period of cental abdominal pain followed by a pain in the right iliac fossa. There is malaise, loss of appetite and change in bowel habit. In addition there are fevers, rigors, sweating.

U Answers

1 a. = 4   b. = 3   c. = 3   d. = 6   e. = 5   f. = 2

2 a. = 2   b. = 3   c. = 3   d. = 1   e. = 5   f. = 5
Not much is known about IgD, although it is a monomer present in B-cells and is involved in B-cell activation. IgG levels fall at 3-6 months which can make the patient prone to infections.

3 a. = 4   b. = 4   c. = 2   d. = 1   e. = 3   f. = 2   g. = 3   h. = 3

4 a. = 3   b. = 4   c. = 2   d. = 1

5 a. = 2   b. = 4   c. = 9   d. = 8   e. = 4   f. = 6   g. = 5   h. = 7

6 a. = 5   b. = 1   c. = 2   d. = 2   e. = 3   f. = 4

7 a. = 7   b. = 1   c. = 1   d. = 4   e. = 5   f. = 7
GGT may also be raised in cholestasis but more often than not ALP is a more significant marker of this.

8 a. = 5   b. = 2   c. = 3

9 a. = 5   b. = 2   c. = 6   d. = 3   e. = 8   f. = 10
Electophysiological studies involve stimulation of the myocardium with electrodes introduced via a cardiac catheter. Other sensors can pick up electrical signals from adjacent myocardium and abberrant conduction pathways can be detected. A patent foramen ovale (PFO) is a persistent communication between the left and right atria. It is not uncommon but often asymptomatic. The bubble test involves passing a small amount of shaken liquid bubbles intravenously that can pass through the right atrium and because they can be detected by ultrasound they can be seen to pass through to the right atrium if a PFO is present. An event recorder is similar to a 24-hour tape; however rather than recording a continuous cardiogram, it electronically records events of abnormal rhythms over longer time periods and can therefore be more sensitive in picking up

paroxysmal atrial fibrillation. Although echocardiography can demonstrate right ventricular dilatation and, by indirect calculations, estimate pulmonary artery pressure, the only definitive way of measuring pulmonary artery pressure is by transducer via catheterisation into that artery. A large proximal pulmonary embolus can be visualised in the right ventrical or pulmonary trunk on echocardiography.

10 a. = 6   b. = 2   c. = 4   d. = 5   e. = 3

11 a. = 4   b. = 1   c. = 2   d. = 3   e. = 5

12 a. = 1   b. = 2   c. = 3   d. = 5   e. = 4

13 a. = 4   b. = 3   c. = 2   d. = 5   e. = 1

Stem a. describes a presentation of acute aortic dissection. This is a potential complication of Marfan's syndrome. Classical features of Marfan's include "spider-like" fingers (arachnodactyly), long extremities, high-arched palate and upward lens dislocation. Expiration increases the intensity of left-sided murmurs.

14 a. = 3   b. = 1   c. = 4   d. = 5   e. = 9   f. = 8

DC cardioversion can be used for supraventricular tachycardias including SVT and AF, as well as ventricular tachycardias and ventricular fibrillation. However, all except for the last example, have other treatment options that can be considered e.g. VT can be treated with antiarrhythmics although it is shocked when pulseless.

15 a. = 3   b. = 4   c. = 1   d. = 5   e. = 2

16 a. = 1   b. = 1   c. = 2   d. = 3   e. = 4   f. = 2   g. = 1

The fourth heart sound is always pathological, and the third heart sound can be normal or pathological. The fourth heart sound is caused by atrial contraction against a stiff left ventricle.

17 a. = 5   b. = 2   c. = 1   d. = 4   e. = 4   f. = 3

18 a. = 7   b. = 2   c. = 3   d. = 1   e. = 1

19 a. = 4   b. = 1   c. = 2   d. = 5   e. = 3

20 a. = 3   b. = 5   c. = 4   d. = 4   e. = 5
Corrigan's sign is prominent carotid pulsation, de Musset's sign is head nodding and Quincke's sign is pulsations seen in the nailbed. All can occur in aortic regurgitation.

21 a. = 5   b. = 5   c. = 3   d. = 2   e. = 1
Eisenmenger's syndrome is the reversal of left to right shunt due to development of pulmonary hypertension and occurs in VSD, ASD and PDA. Clinical features are central cyanosis, clubbing, decreasing intensity of murmurs due to reduced flow and pulmonary hypertension.

22 a. = 5   b. = 2   c. = 9   d. = 8   e. = 7
Shortness of breath with or without pleuritic chest pain should always prompt the doctor to think of PE. In stem c. features which are risk factors for PE include neoplasia and ascites (which obstructs venous return and promotes venous stasis), and likely immobility. Also bear in mind particular haematological malignancies may lead to a hypercoagulable state.

23 a. = 7   b. = 9   c. = 1   d. = 5   e. = 10

24 a. = 2   b. = 1   c. = 4   d. = 3

25 a. = 6   b. = 5   c. = 2   d. = 3   e. = 1   f. = 4

26 a. = 10   b. = 9   c. = 6   d. = 1   e. = 8
Although acne vulgaris is very common, its differential diagnosis must always be considered especially if conventional treatment is not working.

27 a. = 3   b. = 2   c. = 4   d. = 5   e. = 6

28 a. = 5   b. = 4   c. = 1   d. = 3   e. = 3

29 a. = 7   b. = 1   c. = 4   d. = 6   e. = 5   f. = 10

30 a. = 6   b. = 1   c. = 3   d. = 9   e. = 7   f. = 2
Acanthosis nigricans is a black thickening of the skin often seen in the axilla. It is associated with pancreatic cancer, as well as a raised IGF-1 in acromegaly. Necrobiosis lipoidica is a large well-defined patch of waxy sometimes yellow skin with superficial telangiectasia more commonly noted on the legs.

31 a. = 2   b. = 7   c. = 8   d. = 9   e. = 6

32 a. = 4   b. = 2   c. = 5   d. = 6   e. = 10

33 a. = 4   b. = 3   c. = 2   d. = 1   e. = 1

34 a. = 4   b. = 6   c. = 7   d. = 8   e. = 1

35 a. = 3   b. = 2   c. = 3   d. = 1   e. = 2   f. = 4
A rodent ulcer is a BCC, not a melanoma.

36 a. = 3   b. = 7   c. = 1   d. = 2   e. = 9

37 a. = 3   b. = 2   c. = 9   d. = 4   e. = 6
This question is an example of a test of your ability to discriminate possible responses from the most appropriate responses since for each case several options may be correct but only one is the best. For example, the definitive test for MC is electron microscopy. However it is most often diagnosed on clinical inspection and cryotherapy spray may aid diagnosis in difficult cases by highlighting the surface of the lesion to reveal its central umbilication.

38 a. = 5   b. = 3   c. = 6   d. = 1   e. = 7
The most appropriate formulation depends on the site and type of rash. For acute rashes a lotion or cream is better. For a chronic dry scaly rash, an ointment is better. Patients don't like greasy regimens on the face, but prefer creams.

39 a. = 2   b. = 3   c. = 1   d. = 1   e. = 3   f. = 4
It is important to use an appropriate strength steroid. This will help balance the benefit of resolving the condition against the risk of deleterious effects to the skin e.g. thinning and systemic absoption which will be more common where the skin is inflamed.

40 a. = 8   b. = 1   c. = 7   d. = 5   e. = 2
Trichotillomania is a neurotic disorder whereby a patient pulls out their own hair. For this reason, irregular patches of hair loss are seen but, with no underlying skin disorder, new hairs will also be seen in that region.

41 a. = 3   b. = 6   c. = 1   d. = 4

42 a. = 10   b. = 9   c. = 7   d. = 5   e. = 3

43 a. = 7   b. = 9   c. = 2   d. = 8   e. = 1
Formication is the sensation of insects running over or under the skin.

44 a. = 5   b. = 7   c. = 4   d. = 3   e. = 2

45 a. = 3   b. = 6   c. = 1   d. = 4   e. = 10   f. = 7

46 a. = 2   b. = 7   c. = 5   d. = 9   e. = 8

47 a. = 3   b. = 4   c. = 1   d. = 2

48 a. = 1   b. = 5   c. = 7   d. = 5   e. = 6

49 a. = 5   b. = 1   c. = 2   d. = 6   e. = 4

50 a. = 2   b. = 4   c. = 1   d. = 2   e. = 3   f. = 1   g. = 3

51 a. = 2   b. = 3   c. = 3   d. = 3   e. = 3

52 a. = 2   b. = 4   c. = 5   d. = 7   e. = 6

53 a. = 7   b. = 3   c. = 1   d. = 2

54 a. = 4   b. = 5   c. = 1   d. = 5

55 a. = 4   b. = 6   c. = 6   d. = 9   e. = 1

56 a. = 3   b. = 6   c. = 7   d. = 5   e. = 1

57 a. = 4   b. = 5   c. = 2   d. = 1   e. = 4
Bezoar is the medical term for food, fiber, mucus, etc that cannot be digested by the stomach.

58 a. = 1   b. = 3   c. = 9   d. = 6   e. = 7

59 a. = 6   b. = 4   c. = 1   d. = 5   e. = 9

60 a. = 3   b. = 5   c. = 4   d. = 2   e. = 9

61   a. = 6   b. = 7   c. = 8   d. = 1   e. = 6

62   a. = 2   b. = 3   c. = 1   d. = 1   e. = 1

63   a. = 5   b. = 4   c. = 8   d. = 2   e. = 2

Singer's nodes is caused by misuse of the voice and bad voice production, often in the presence of inflammation and is common in school children (screamers) and actors, teachers and singers.

64   a. = 3   b. = 4   c. = 2   d. = 2   e. = 1

65   a. = 4   b. = 5   c. = 1   d. = 5   e. = 7

66   a. = 4   b. = 3   c. = 2   d. = 1   e. = 7   f. = 1

ESR is classically a useful marker for temporal arteritis. However the CRP is also very useful, particularly in monitoring response to treatment.

67   a. = 7   b. = 8   c. = 10   d. = 5   e. = 4

Pellagra is vitamin B3 (niacin) deficiency and scurvy is vitamin C deficiency.

68   a. = 3   b. = 4   c. = 7   d. = 8   e. = 2

69   a. = 8   b. = 1   c. = 6   d. = 3

Crohn's disease tends to be rectal sparing.

70   a. = 6   b. = 2   c. = 4   d. = 6   e. = 4

71   a. = 2   b. = 5   c. = 5   d. = 4   e. = 1   f. = 6   g. = 4

In these situations the patient is likely to have diarrhoea, decreased weight and steatorrhoea (offensive smelling stools that do not flush easily). They may have bleeding problems due to low vitamin K, oedema from low protein, and signs of anaemia (pale, short of breath, light-headedness and malaise), due to lack of iron, vitamin B12 and folate. For Giardia, the mechanism of malabsorption is not clearly understood, yet it is thought to be more complicated than simple infection or bacterial overgrowth and disruption of nutrient transfer across the gut wall is implicated.

72   a. = 3   b. = 4   c. = 2   d. = 3   e. = 1

73 a. = 8   b. = 5   c. = 9   d. = 4

74 a. = 10   b. = 1   c. = 9   d. = 8

75 a. = 1   b. = 6   c. = 7   d. = 2   e. = 8

76 a. = 6   b. = 4   c. = 5   d. = 7   e. = 3
The prognosis in acute pancreatitis may be measured using the Glasgow criteria (which are validated for use in both alcoholic and gallstone induced pancreatitis) and Ranson's criteria (for use only in alcohol induced pancreatitis). Neither of these criteria include amylase as a prognostic marker.

77 a. = 5   b. = 3   c. = 2   d. = 7   e. = 1   f. = 7   g. = 4   h. = 2
Philadelphia chromosome is a balanced translocation between chromosomes 9 and 22.

78 a. = 3   b. = 3   c. = 1   d. = 2   e. = 2
Prothrombin time measures the extrinsic sytem and the final common pathway - increased with warfarin.
Activated partial thromboplastin time - measures intrinsic and final common pathways, increased with heparin,
Thrombin time - measures the final part of the common pathway

79 a. = 3   b. = 7   c. = 1   d. = 6

80 a. = 4   b. = 5   c. = 8   d. = 2   e. = 3   f. = 6   g. = 7

81 a. = 3   b. = 3   c. = 1   d. = 2   e. = 5

82 a. = 8   b. = 7   c. = 6   d. = 5   e. = 7   f. = 8
MMR is not contraindicated in those allergic to eggs, read the BNF.

83 a. = 3   b. = 10   c. = 4   d. = 1   e. = 7

84 a. = 1   b. = 6   c. = 3   d. = 5

85 a. = 5   b. = 1   c. = 4   d. = 3

86 a. = 2   b. = 5   c. = 5   d. = 5   e. = 4   f. = 3   g. = 3   h. = 3

87   a. = 2   b. = 10   c. = 8   d. = 5   e. = 2   f. = 6   g. = 7   h. = 9

88   a. = 3   b. = 6   c. = 5   d. = 3   e. = 1   f. = 2   g. = 6

89   a. = 3   b. = 7   c. = 9   d. = 10   e. = 1   f. = 2

90   a. = 1   b. = 3   c. = 6   d. = 5   e. = 5

91   a. = 6   b. = 4   c. = 4   d. = 2   e. = 1   f. = 1   g. = 1

92   a. = 7   b. = 5   c. = 2   d. = 4   e. = 1

93   a. = 6   b. = 7   c. = 8   d. = 4   e. = 10   f. = 5

94   a. = 1   b. = 3   c. = 3   d. = 2   e. = 2   f. = 2   g. = 2
It is important to read the question and not get confused with simple nausea and vomitting and the clinical condition hyperemesis gravidarum.

95   a. = 4   b. = 3   c. = 7   d. = 1   e. = 2

96   a. = 1   b. = 3   c. = 4   d. = 2   e. = 6

97   a. = 1   b. = 6   c. = 7   d. = 3   e. = 5   f. = 4
Pearl index is a measure of the chance of getting pregnant if a 100 woman took these contraceptive measures for one year.

98   a. = 3   b. =4   c. =7   d. =1   e. =9   f. =2   g. =1   h. =5
Persona ® is a computerised device that can indicate "safe periods" during a woman's menstrual cycle when sexual intercourse is unlikely to lead to pregnancy. It is calibrated by using urine samples but its suitability is restricted to younger women with regular cycles amongst other constraints.

99   a. = 7   b. = 5   c. = 4   d. = 4   e. = 3

100   a. = 10   b. = 6   c. = 4   d. = 4   e. = 2

101   a. = 5   b. = 4   c. = 6   d. = 1   e. = 2   f. = 4   g. = 4

102   a. = 1   b. = 3   c. = 2   d. = 2   e. = 1

103 a. = 2   b. = 4   c. = 4   d. = 3   e. = 1

104 a. = 1   b. = 3   c. = 4   d. = 2   e. = 7

105 a. = 1   b. = 4   c. = 7   d. = 2   e. = 8

106 a. = 6   b. = 7   c. = 4   d. = 3   e. = 8

107 a. = 1   b. = 9   c. = 2   d. = 3   e. = 8   f. = 8   g. = 1
The association of IgA deficiency with carcinoma of the stomach is mainly theoretical.

108 a. = 6   b. = 6   c. = 6   d. = 3   e. = 1

109 a. = 9   b. = 1   c. = 8   d. = 3   e. = 5   f. = 4   g. = 7

110 a. = 2   b. = 3   c. = 2   d. = 6   e. = 3   f. = 3   g. = 4

111 a. = 5   b. = 4   c. = 3   d. = 1   e. = 3

112 a. = 5   b. = 4   c. = 4   d. = 3   e. = 1

113 a. = 7   b. = 8   c. = 9   d. = 3   e. = 1

114 a. = 5   b. = 7   c. = 7   d. = 2   e. = 1   f. = 2

115 a. = 2   b. = 3   c. = 1   d. = 4   e. = 7

116 a. = 10   b. = 9   c. = 8   d. = 5   e. = 4

117 a. = 6   b. = 4   c. = 3   d. = 2   e. = 8

118 a. = 10   b. = 9   c. = 8   d. = 7   e. = 3   f. = 4   g. = 2

119 a. = 7   b. = 8   c. = 9   d. = 1   e. = 2   f. = 3

120 a. = 6   b. = 2   c. = 7   d. = 10   e. = 4   f. = 3

121 a. = 10   b. = 8   c. = 7   d. = 5

122 a. = 4   b. = 4   c. = 5   d. = 2   e. = 1   f. = 1   g. = 1

123 a. = 10   b. = 8   c. = 5   d. = 4   e. = 3

Sturge-Weber syndrome is an association of a port wine stain on the face in the distribution of the trigeminal nerve with focal fits from a contralateral cranial capillary haemangioma.

124 a. = 2   b. = 1   c. = 3   d. = 5   e. = 7   f. = 6

Occulomucocutaneous syndrome affects the skin, eyes and mucous membranes. Patients complain of hot, gritty eyes and photophobia due to a reduction in tear flow.

125 a. = 9   b. = 7   c. = 7   d. = 8   e. = 4   f. = 3

126 a. = 3   b. = 2   c. = 5   d. = 7   e. = 6

Ocular examination of a patient with amaurosis fugax may be normal or retinal emboli may be visible. Possible causes of amaurosis fugax include carotid artery disease, emboli from the heart, intravenous drug abuse and temporal arteritis.

127 a. = 2   b. = 10   c. = 6   d. = 8   e. = 9

128 a. = 9   b. = 6   c. = 2   d. = 4   e. = 10

Other associated connective tissue diseases with scleritis are ankylosing spondylitis, systemic lupus erythematous and systemic vasculitis.

The symptoms of acanthamoeba keratitis are often more severe than the clinical presentation would suggest. It is important to educate patients about the dangers of swimming or washing their contact lenses with tap water.

129 a. = 5   b. = 7   c. = 10   d. = 3   e. = 4

To confirm diagnosis of Holmes-Adie pupil, a solution of 0.125% pilocarpine is instilled in each eye. The Holmes-Adie pupil will constrict to the weak pilocarpine. With time, this pupil may become more miotic and may actually become smaller than the normal pupil. These ocular signs in association with absent knee and ankle reflexes are known as the Holmes-Adie syndrome. *Atropa belladonna* or Deadly Nightshade is one of the most toxic plants in the western hemisphere and its side effects are due to atropine poisoning.

130 a. = 9   b. = 7   c. = 2   d. = 1   e. = 6

Heterochromic iridis, in which the iris on the affected side is less pigmented is associated with congenital Horner's syndrome.

131 a. = 3   b. = 8   c. = 9   d. = 4   e. = 7
The ring of brown pigment is the Fleischer ring. Treatment for keratoconus is with the use of spectacles to correct visual acuity. Rigid gas permeable lenses are particularly useful to treat advanced cases. Penetrating keratoplasty can be performed when vision can no longer be corrected by either spectacles or contact lenses.

132 a. = 1   b. = 7   c. = 2   d. = 8   e. = 3
Soft tissue signs in thyroid eye disease result from retro-orbital inflammation and lymphocytic infiltration with swelling and fibrosis of extra-ocular muscles. These soft tissue signs are only seen in Graves' and not in any other form of thyroid disease.

133 a. = 4   b. = 8   c. = 5   d. = 7   e. = 2
Angoid streaks are due to abnornmalities in the Bruch membrane of the retina. As well as the haemoglobinopathies, they may be found in a number of conditions including pseudoxanthoma elasticum, Paget's disease and Ehlers-Danlos, or they may be idiopathic. Homocystinuria gives a similar phenotype to Marfan's syndrome but there is downward lens dislocation, osteoporosis, recurrent thrombosis and reduced IQ.

134 a. = 1   b. = 4   c. = 5   d. = 2
In ophthalmoplegic shingles, involvement of the tip of the nose (Hutchinson's sign) indicates involvement of the nasociliary branch of the trigeminal nerve. This also innervates the globe therefore making eye involvement likely. Specialist referral for slit lamp examination is essential.

Talbot's test is positive if a patient reports eye pain when their pupils constrict as their eyes converge on an object (i.e. when a patient follows a finger approaching their nose). For this question, this will diagnose acute iritis in this instance. Cyclopentolate is used to keep the pupil dilated to prevent adhesions forming between the lens and iris. If steroid drops are being considered for any condition, slit lamp examination should be performed to exclude dendritic ulcers at the outset.

135 a. = 6   b. = 7   c. = 1   d. = 2   e. = 4   f. = 5   g. = 6
Corneal arcus may be a sign of hyperlipidaemia, or may be an incidental finding, especially in the elderly.

136 a. = 4   b. = 2   c. = 2   d. = 1   e. = 3   f. = 3   g. = 3
Silver wiring may also be referred to as copper wiring.

137 a. = 7   b. = 6   c. = 8   d. = 2   e. = 4   f. = 1   g. = 1   h. = 1
45-80% of those with optic neuritis develop multiple sclerosis over the next 15 years.

138 a. = 5   b. = 9   c. = 10   d. = 2   e. = 1

139 a. = 9   b. = 5   c. = 8   d. = 6   e. = 7
Rheumatoid arthritis also affects the soft tissues, for example causing tenosynovitis which may lead to tendon rupture (commonly extensor more than flexor tendons) or carpal tunnel syndrome. Rheumatoid arthritis may also cause ligament laxity, for example leading to the dangerous complication of atlanto-axial subluxation.

140 a. = 6   b. = 4   c. = 2   d. = 3   e. = 4

141 a. = 3   b. = 1   c. = 5   d. = 4   e. = 1   f. = 2
The toes in pes cavus may be clawed. Pes cavus is noted in conditions where there is weakness of the intrinsic muscles of the foot. This results in contraction or arching of the foot and may also lead to clawing of the toes. Conditions associated with pes cavus include hereditary neurological disorders such as Charcot-Marie-Tooth syndrome or Friedreich's ataxia.

142 a. = 4   b. = 5   c. = 1   d. = 2   e. = 2   f. = 1
Osteochondritis or softening and deformity of bone can lead to foot pain in both children and adolescents.

143 a. = 4   b. = 2   c. = 5   d. = 3   e. = 1
Compound fractures occur when a fracture is open to the air through a skin wound. All are at high risk of infection. A grade I fracture has <2% infection risk whereas a grade III has >10% infection risk.

144 a. = 3   b. = 1   c. = 1   d. = 2   e. = 4
If a Colles' fracture is displaced, it gives a characteristic 'dinner-fork' deformity to the hand and wrist.

145 a. = 1   b. = 4   c. = 2   d. = 3
Hip fractures are very common, especially among elderly ladies suffering from osteoporosis and must be suspected. It is associated with a significant mortality. In a stage III fracture, the fragments are held together by the posterior retinaculum allowing partial displacement and misalignment of the femoral trabeculae.

146 a. = 2   b. = 5   c. = 2   d. = 3   e. = 4   f. = 5

In acute asthma, the pCO_2 is usually slightly low owing to the increased respiratory rate and relative rapidity of transfer of CO_2 compared to O_2; a normalising pCO_2 may indicate an increasingly severe episode, and an elevated pCO_2 is very worrying.

147 a. = 2   b. = 2   c. = 6   d. = 1   e. = 7

A pseudo-Bartter's syndrome may be seen in cystic fibrosis. Dehydration may also present with normal or low sodium. There is a significant total body deficit of potassium in DKA, despite initial hyperkalaemia.

148 a. = 4   b. = 1   c. = 3   d. = 4   e. = 8   f. = 9

149 a. = 10   b. = 9   c. = 5   d. = 7   e. = 4

150 a. = 8   b. = 4   c. = 2   d. = 4   e. = 6

151 a. = 10   b. = 7   c. = 3   d. = 1   e. = 4   f. = 5

152 a. = 1   b. = 9   c. = 5   d. = 4   e. = 3

153 a. = 8   b. = 2   c. = 4   d. = 7   e. = 1

154 a. = 5   b. = 3   c. = 1   d. = 7   e. = 6

155 a. = 5   b. = 3   c. = 2   d. = 7   e. = 1

156 a. = 6   b. = 7   c. = 9   d. = 2   e. = 8

157 a. = 8   b. = 7   c. = 5   d. = 1   e. = 4

It is important to distinguish between innocent murmurs and pathological murmurs. Innocent murmurs have no clinical significance, are systolic and musical and do not radiate. They vary with posture and position.

158 a. = 5   b. = 6   c. = 7   d. = 1   e. = 4

159 a. = 1   b. = 3   c. = 4   d. = 2

160 a. = 2   b. = 5   c. = 6

Prolonged jaundice (over 2 weeks) should be referred to paediatrics for evaluation to exclude serious treatable conditions such as hypothyroidism and biliary atresia. The vast majority of such children will have breastfeeding jaundice.

161 a. = 8   b. = 3   c. = 6   d. = 7   e. = 9

162 a. = 9   b. = 7   c. = 5   d. = 4   e. = 2   f. = 1

163 a. = 10   b. = 5   c. = 9   d. = 1   e. = 2

164 a. = 3   b. = 4   c. = 5   d. = 6   e. = 7

165 a. = 2   b. = 3   c. = 5   d. = 6   e. = 9

166 a. = 8   b. = 2   c. = 3   d. = 3
Don't forget to step down as well as step up once good control has been maintained for some time.

167 a. = 2   b. = 6   c. = 5   d. = 3   e. = 1
The mothers and siblings of children with rickets may also require treatment with Vitamin D.

168 a. = 3   b. = 5   c. = 10   d. = 7   e. = 2
You must know all the components of the Apgar score - Heart rate, respiration, muscle tone, irritability and colour.

169 a. = 4   b. = 6   c. = 2   d. = 7   e. = 9

170 a. = 6   b. = 2   c. = 3   d. = 7   e. = 9

171 a. = 5   b. = 6   c. = 4   d. = 3   e. = 2   f. = 2   g. = 1

172 a. = 7   b. = 3   c. = 4   d. = 2   e. = 9

173 a. = 5   b. = 8   c. = 1   d. = 3   e. = 9   f. = 2

174 a. = 1   b. = 1   c. = 2   d. = 3   e. = 4   f. = 5
Febrile convulsions occur in 5% of children and are very rarely associated with epilepsy in later life. Risk is increased if febrile convulsions are atypical.

175 a. = 1   b. = 3   c. = 4   d. = 2
Although it is vitally important to think of and act in suspected cases, non-accidental injury is still thankfully a rare diagnosis.

176 a. = 3   b. = 6   c. = 10   d. = 1   e. = 2
Aspirin stops platelet aggregation and is used in primary and secondary prevention of cardiovascular disease. Clopidrogel also stops platelet aggregation but by interfering with its ADP receptor sites and can be used in conjunction with or, in cases of aspirin intolerance, instead of aspirin.

177 a. = 5   b. = 4   c. = 6   d. = 6   e. = 7   f. = 8

178 a. = 3   b. = 8   c. = 6   d. = 10   e. = 1

179 a. = 3   b. = 3   c. = 1   d. = 1   e. = 2
In practical terms it takes longer for enzymes to be induced than to be inhibited. Short courses of antibiotics are common circumstances when these interactions must be thought through and a little extra thought – for instance requesting more frequent INRs for a warfarin patient or advising barrier contraception for those on the combined contraceptive pill – may be all that is required.

180 a. = 9   b. = 3   c. = 6   d. = 2   e. = 10   f. = 8   g. = 1

181 a. = 8   b. = 3   c. = 5   d. = 1   e. = 2   f. = 3   g. = 9   h. = 3

182 a. = 5   b. = 4   c. = 4   d. = 2   e. = 1   f. = 7   g. = 8   h. = 3

183 a. = 9   b. = 6   c. = 7   d. = 3   e. = 1   f. = 4   g. = 8
Fentanyl lozenges can be easily absorbed via the buccal mucosa to give a fast strong effect, yet can be just as easily spat out to terminate this. This is ideal for the "incident" pain described in stem a. Whilst options 1, 3, 5 and 7 may all be considered for stem b, diclofrenac is noted to be particularly effective for renal colic but can also be given as a suppository, which is ideal for a patient who may be nil by mouth. Codydramol is a widely used weak opioid, easy to use and safe as an oral analgesic at home. Diamorphine is classically administered during acute cardiac events for analgesia but also causes vasodilatation, which is of benefit. Gabapentin which has less side effects than amitriptyline can also be used for neuropathic pain.

184 a. = 6   b. = 2   c. = 1   d. = 1   e. = 4   f. = 4

185 a. = 7   b. = 2   c. = 3   d. = 5   e. = 2   f. = 6   g. = 4

186 a. = 4   b. = 4   c. = 5   d. = 2   e. = 1   f. = 1   g = 4

187 a. = 5   b. = 5   c. = 4   d. = 2   e. = 3   e. = 2   g = 1

188 a. = 8   b. = 9   c. = 3   d. = 5   e. = 4   f. = 7   g. = 2

189 a. = 5   b. = 9   c. = 1   d. = 9   e. = 7   f. = 8

190 a. = 4   b. = 6   c. = 2   d. = 1   e. = 5

191 a. = 9   b. = 4   c. = 6   d. = 1   e. = 2   f. = 3   g. = 6   h. = 4
Pabrinex® is a mixture of vitamin C and B vitamins which is given i.m., whereas thiamine (B_1) alone is continued orally in some patients. Pyridoxine (B_6) is given alongside isoniazid therapy to reduce the risk of peripheral neuropathy.

192 a. = 3   b. = 5   c. = 2   d. = 1   e. = 1

193 a. = 6   b. = 5   c. = 1   d. = 1   e. = 1   f. = 5

194 a. = 9   b. = 6   c. = 1   d. = 5   e. = 6

195 a. = 3   b. = 1   c. = 7   d. = 9   e. = 4

196 a. = 2   b. = 2   c. = 6   d. = 1   e. = 3

197 a. = 3   b. = 1   c. = 4   d. = 3   e. = 2   f. = 3
Although potency varies along this scale, it is an exponential scale as opposed to a linear scale.

198 a. = 5   b. = 4   c. = 1   d. = 3   e. = 6   f. = 6   g. = 7

199 a. = 8   b. = 7   c. = 5   d. = 4   e. = 3

200 a. = 6   b. = 7   c. = 9   d. = 10   e. = 5

201 a. = 7   b. = 6   c. = 3   d. = 4   e. = 6

202 a. = 6   b. = 7   c. = 8   d. = 3   e. = 4

203 a. = 8   b. = 10   c. = 2   d. = 7   e. = 6
Psychiatric disorders may be provoked by or influenced by factors in their social environment.

204 a. = 9   b. = 10   c. = 6   d. = 3   e. = 2

205 a. = 8   b. = 6   c. = 2   d. = 7   e. = 3

206 a. = 4   b. = 5   c. = 6   d. = 1   e. = 2

207 a. = 6   b. = 4   c. = 1   d. = 2   e. = 8

208 a. = 2   b. = 1   c. = 4   d. = 7   e. = 4

209 a. = 2   b. = 1   c. = 8   d. = 10   e. = 2   f. = 6   g. = 8

210 a. = 5   b. = 2   c. = 4

211 a. = 5   b. = 1   c. = 4   d. = 3

212 a. = 4   b. = 7   c. = 5   d. = 1   e. = 3

213 a. = 1   b. = 3   c. = 3   d. = 2   e. = 2

214 a. = 3   b. = 2   c. = 2   d. = 4   e. = 5

215 a. = 7   b. = 9   c. = 3   d. = 6   e. = 1

216 a. = 2   b. = 6   c. = 8   d. = 9   e. = 10

217 a. = 4   b. = 7   c. = 7   d. = 5   e = 9
Plain abdominal films look at the renal outlines, situated at T12-L2. 90% of renal stones are radio-opaque. They may also demonstrate calcified neoplasms, tuberculosis or nephrocalcinosis.

218 a. = 5   b. = 6   c. = 4   d. = 1   e. = 1   f. = 4
The pathology of glomerulonephritis is complex. Focal means some of the glomeruli are affected. Diffuse means all are affected. Segmental means part of each glomerulus is affected.

219 a. = 3   b. = 8   c. = 5   d. = 6   e. = 9   f. = 4   g. = 4
Haemolytic uraemic syndrome (HUS) is an overlapping syndrome with thrombotic thrombocytopenic purpura (TTP) but has the predominant symptom of renal dysfunction. HUS frequently affects children. In TTP, cerebral dysfunction is more common and tends to affect adults. Haemolytic uraemic syndrome may be caused by verotoxin producing strains of *E. coli*.

220 a. = 3   b. = 2   c. = 1   d. = 5
Alport's is inherited as an X-linked dominant syndrome. The eye lesions include retinal flecks, lenticonus and cataracts.

221 a. = 10   b. = 8   c. = 5   d. = 6

222 a. = 4   b. = 1   c. = 3   d. = 2   e. = 5
Incontinence is a common condition, but the symptoms are not easily volunteered. Once a urinary tract infection and diabetes have been excluded, urodynamic studies will help distinguish between stress and urge incontinence. Urge incontinence or detrusor instability may respond to bladder training, restricting fluid intake and antimuscarinic drugs. Mild stress incontinence may respond to pelvic floor exercises but more severe cases may require surgical intervention.

223 a. = 9   b. = 3   c. = 2   d. = 6   e. = 1   f. = 7   g. = 4

224 a. = 3   b. = 4   c. = 1   d. = 2   e. = 5
Chronic obstructive pulmonary disease (COPD) encompasses both chronic bronchitis and emphysema and is now the preferred term (as stated in NICE guidelines). It is characterised by airway obstruction with little or no reversibility.

225 a. = 1   b. = 5   c. = 6   d. = 3

226 a. = 2   b. = 1   c. = 3   d. = 4
Predicted lung volumes are dependent on age, gender, height and ethnicity. In obstructive defects such as COPD, FEV_1 is reduced more than FVC, therefore the FEV_1/FVC ratio will be <75%. In restrictive defects such as pulmonary fibrosis, both FEV_1 and FVC are reduced and the ratio either remains normal or is increased.

227 a. = 3   b. = 1   c. = 4   d. = 2   e. = 6
Changing lifestyle is very difficult to do, but a GP has a key role in this. Stopping smoking is the best lifestyle choice for a patient with COPD.

228 a. = 4   b. = 5   c. = 2   d. = 1   e. = 1

229 a. = 4   b. = 3   c. = 1   d. = 5   e. = 4   f. = 5   g. = 6   h. = 7
Kartagener's syndrome is characterised by ciliary immotility leading to chronic sinusitis, bronchiectasis and infertility plus dextrocardia and situs inversus.

230 a. = 2   b. = 5   c. = 3   d. = 3   e. = 1   f = 4
The British Thoracic Society Guidelines for managing asthma suggest starting at the highest step needed to control the severity of the asthma and then moving down if control remains good for >3 months. Rescue courses of oral prednisolone may be added in at any step as required.

231 a. = 1   b. = 8   c. = 2   d. = 1   e. = 3
The fumes from molten beryllium may cause an acute alveolitis. However chronic beryllium exposure leads to a progressive granulomatous lung disease similar to sarcoidosis. Baritosis is due to exposure to barium.

232 a. = 3   b. = 1   c. = 2   d. = 7
These types of question assess your ability to problem solve in a clinical situation and are a common type of exam question.

233 a. = 1   b. = 2   c. = 5   d. = 4

234 a. = 1   b. = 4   c. = 3   d. = 5   e. = 2

235 a. = 3   b. = 3   c. = 7   d. = 5   e. = 3
Important to know the difference between haematemesis and haemoptysis and get a clear history from the patient.

236 a. = 3   b. = 2   c. = 2   d. = 3   e. = 1   f. = 3   g. = 3

237 a. = 2   b. = 1   c. = 2   d. = 2   e. = 3   f. = 4
Lesch-Nyhan syndrome is an inherited disorder of purine synthesis leading to gout, renal failure, self-mutilation and central nervous system signs.

238 a. = 6   b. = 4   c. = 1   d. = 4   e. = 1
The spondyloarthropathies include ankylosing spondylitis, psoriatic arthropathy, enteropathic arthritis (associated with inflammatory bowel disease) and Reiter's or reactive arthritis. They are all seronegative (i.e. rheumatoid factor negative) and there is an association with HLA-B27. SLE and systemic sclerosis are not spondyloarthropathies.

239 a. = 7   b. = 1   c. = 5   d. = 6   e. = 6
CREST stands for C=calcinosis R=Raynaud's E=oesophageal involvement S=sclerodactaly T=telangectasia.
Mixed connective tissue disease combines features of systemic lupus erythematosus, polymyositis and systemic sclerosis.

240 a. = 6   b. = 7   c. = 2   d. = 2   e. = 1   f. = 5
The top four antibodies are also present in SLE.

241 a. = 4   b. = 5   c. = 1   d. = 1
Thoracic outlet syndrome involves the lower trunk of the brachial plexus and the subclavian artery. Pain and parasthaesia are typically felt along the ulnar border of the forearm and wrist. There may be wasting and weakness of the intrinsic muscles of the hand and the radial pulse may be weak.

242 a. = 2   b. = 3   c. = 5   d. = 5   e. = 4
A painful arc is pain on abduction between 45-160°. This may be seen in partial rotator cuff tears, supraspinatus tendonitis, calcifying tendonitis or acromioclavicular joint osteoarthritis. Axillary nerve damage in an anterior shoulder dislocation may lead to this sensory loss and deltoid paralysis.

243 a. = 4   b. = 7   c. = 10   d. = 1   e. = 6

244 a. = 4   b. = 3   c. = 8   d. = 10   e. = 5

245 a. = 5   b. = 1   c. = 6   d. = 3   e. = 1

246 a. = 6   b. = 3   c. = 1   d. = 3   e. = 7   f. = 4   g. = 7   h. = 8

247 a. = 3   b. = 5   c. = 4   d. = 8   e. = 10

248 a. = 3   b. = 1   c. = 2   d. = 4

249 a. = 6   b. = 7   c. = 4   d. = 2   e. = 2   f. = 1

250 a. = 10   b. = 9   c. = 8   d. = 4   e. = 2

251 a. = 2   b. = 8   c. = 4   d. = 7   e. = 5
Ectopic functionning gastric tissue can occasionally be found in Meckel's diverticulae.

252 a. = 3   b. = 4   c. = 6   d. = 2   e. = 2

253 a. = 4   b. = 1   c. = 3   d. = 2   e. = 3

254 a. = 3   b. = 4   c. = 1   d. = 1   e. = 3
There are four types of thyroid cancer. They have similar clinical features but differ in their prognosis and treatment options.

255 a. = 5   b. = 6   c. = 3   d. = 2   e. = 8   f. = 7

256 a. = 6   b. = 1   c. = 2   d. = 4   e. = 3   f. = 5

257 a. = 3   b. = 6   c. = 2   d. = 8

258 a. = 9   b. = 4   c. = 8   d. = 1   e. = 2

OTHER BOOKS IN THIS SERIES

GPST STAGE 2 – Clinical Problem Solving
300 MCQs (Single Best Answer) for GPST / GPVTS entry
4th edition: ISBN 978-1-905812-20-2
Nishali Patel, David Phillips

GPST STAGE 2 – Professional Dilemmas
100 scenarios for GPST / GPVTS entry
4th edition: ISBN 978-1-905812-22-6
Olivier Picard, Gail Allsopp

GPST STAGE 3 – Selection Centre
Ultimate Guide to the GPST / GPVTS selection centre
4th edition: ISBN 978-1-905812-23-3
Gail Allsopp